Critical Guides to French Texts

KU-222-599

120 Corneille: Cinna

Critical Guides to French Texts
EDITED BY ROGER LITTLE, WOLFGANG VAN EMDEN, DAVID WILLIAMS

CORNEILLE

Cinna

C. J. Gossip

Professor of French
University of New England

Grant & Cutler Ltd
1998

© Grant & Cutler Ltd 1998

ISBN 0 7293 0406 X

T 1001512492

DEPÓSITO LEGAL: V. 3.612 - 1998

Printed in Spain by
Artes Gráficas Soler, S.A., Valencia
for
GRANT & CUTLER LTD
55–57 GREAT MARLBOROUGH STREET, LONDON W1V 2AY

Contents

Preliminary Note

Quotations from Corneille's plays and critical writings are taken from the G. Couton edition (see the Bibliography at the end of this volume, *1*) and are followed in the text by the relevant line number(s) or volume and page reference. The D.A. Watts edition of *Cinna* (*4*) has been used for the indentations mentioned in chapter 2.

Other works referred to are listed and numbered in the Bibliography and are mentioned in the text by means of the relevant italic number, followed where appropriate by a page reference.

1. Structures and Rhythms

As they left the Théâtre du Marais in Paris early one Friday evening in July or August 1642, the several hundred members of the audience which had just seen the first performance of *Cinna* had every right to be excited. Corneille's eleventh play contained a clear, straight-forward plot, a considerable amount of suspense, a dénouement which, if known in outline beforehand, was still surprising in its detail, and a number of well-drawn figures whose aims and beliefs set up numerous clashes of will and intention. If it fitted in with the current fashion for conspiracy and revenge tragedies, it stood out by the simplicity of its structure, its early adherence to the main unities, and the concise forcefulness of most of its dialogue. It is no surprise, then, that *Cinna*, later identified by its author as one of his favourites, went on to have many performances during the rest of his lifetime and has remained one of his most popular, if also most puzzling, works.

While modern theatre audiences or students of Corneille can have ready access to the text, this was not an option for early spectators, since plays in seventeenth-century France were only printed once the initial run of performances was complete, at which time the work fell into the public domain. Until the tragedy appeared in print in January 1643, it was merely through live performances that most Parisians and others could have known it. What was that experience like, and how did contemporary circumstances and conventions impinge on performance? Indeed, why is *Cinna* the play it is, both in form and content, and what has the tragedy to say, both to its initial audiences and to readers today?

The original Marais theatre was a rectangular building which measured internally some 31 metres long, 11.2 metres wide and 16 metres high. After it burned down in 1644, it was rebuilt and the length increased to 34.4 metres. In the new building as probably in the old, the gently inclined stage occupied the full width at one end and was 9.75 metres deep, with the front raised 1.95 metres above the flat floor of the auditorium. The Marais had the shape, and some of the fittings, of a seventeenth-century indoor (real) tennis court, a *jeu de paume,* which is what it was before conversion. As at the rival theatre called the Hôtel de Bourgogne and possibly in the original Marais, some 3.9 metres above the rear half of the new main stage was a second, upper stage or *petit théâtre,* a shelf-like structure supported by pillars on which actions such as the defence of a city's walls or the appearance of a deity could take place. The main playing area on the principal stage was only some 7.8 metres across and 5.8 metres deep, probably slightly shallower in the pre-1644 Marais. Part of the audience sat in galleries and boxes along the two side walls of the building and at the end facing the stage, but others – perhaps the majority at most performances – stood in the level pit or *parterre.* While there is some dispute about the social mix of these 'groundlings', it is clear that most, if not all, were men, women preferring to be seated in safety elsewhere. The design of the theatre, its inadequate sight-lines, the distance between actors and many of the patrons, the poor acoustics, and the commotion which must have reigned in the pit all militated against the reverent hush in which French neoclassical tragedy is played in modern theatres. To add to the problems of a small performance space, from 1637 onwards members of the aristocracy occupied chairs on each side of the stage, reducing the actual playing area, impeding access, and making noisy entrances and exits.

Like his contemporaries, Corneille took these difficult conditions for granted – he knew no other –, but it is important to realise that plays were written with them in mind. If *Cinna* and other tragedies of the period, perhaps especially those dealing with political themes or Roman subjects, seem to us rather bombastic, this is because events were more easily conveyed by words than by physical actions, with the dialogue delivered mainly from the front of the small stage, declaimed rather than spoken naturally. A play dealing with imperial Rome, conspiratorial plotting and political advice-seeking will naturally contain rhetorical elements; but French playwrights of the 1630s and 1640s were well attuned to the various elements of scenes and acts, the *récit,* the soliloquy, dialogue between two or more characters, all expressed in rhyming couplets made up of the twelve-syllable alexandrine line conventional in French tragedy and much comedy.

That *Cinna* was an immediate success and became an enduring masterpiece is due, first and foremost, to its deceptively simple structure, an examination of which may provide the best way in to this dramatic text. What we shall be looking at is the interlocking framework of character meetings and avoidances which together make up the plot or *intrigue*, the sequencing of entrances and exits, the proportions of speech given to various characters, the relationship between principal and minor figures – in short, the building blocks which the dramatist uses to construct his play.

Corneille has five acts in which to tell his tale, and some eighteen hundred lines, for candles which kept both stage and auditorium lit during performances only lasted about half an hour before they had to be changed, making each act of roughly similar length (350-400 lines) a self-contained unit, with the necessary four intervals heightening the division between acts. The dramatist's first problem is not where to end his play, since the pardon which the Emperor Augustus extended to Cinna in the historical accounts provides the obvious dénouement, but rather where to start it. By the early 1640s it was accepted practice for tragedies to adhere to the so-called three unities, of time, place, and action – guidelines suggested by Aristotle in his *Poetics* and refined by sixteenth- and early seventeenth-century playwrights and theorists in France and Italy. The audience attracted to *Cinna* in 1642 expected a plot which occupied at most twenty-four hours of 'historical' time and preferably less (within the three hours or so of 'performance' time), with a setting which was a single town, or more likely a single building within it, and containing events around one main action, with any attendant developments being clearly subsidiary to it.

As we shall see later, Corneille drew his inspiration from an event recounted by Seneca in the first century AD and by the Greek-language historian Cassius Dio, writing in the early third century.

These two versions differ in their detail, but essentially attribute the unexpected clemency to arguments presented by the Emperor's wife Livia Drusilla and accepted unquestioningly by her husband. Corneille will introduce a Livie, offering advice and then praise, but his Auguste angrily rejects her suggestion of pardon. His most important innovation by far, however, is the addition of another two named conspirators – Maxime, a staunch Republican anxious to rid Rome of its new Imperial trappings, and Emilie, a daughter of Auguste's former tutor Toranius and now virtually adopted by Auguste. While Maxime will play an important part, clashing with Cinna and turning out to be his rival in love, it is Emilie's ideas and actions which give a new shape to the old story. For neither Seneca nor Cassius Dio had provided a motive for Cinna's assassination plot. Corneille invents Emilie and makes her a determined, indeed fanatical opponent of the Emperor, who had personally put her father to death. Prior to Cinna's conspiracy there is Emilie's revenge; it is to satisfy this thirst for vengeance that Cinna, head over heels in love with her, agrees to lead the assassination attempt. In interweaving the personal relationships and the political arguments, the short timespan, confined space and rigorous relevance called for by the dramatic unities can be a help rather than a hindrance; but the problems associated with construction and balance still remain.

Corneille chooses to open his tragedy the day before the planned assassination bid. Yet rather than showing Cinna and Maxime finalising the details as the curtain goes up, he offers us Emilie on her own, nursing her wrath but taking time to weigh up her aims and chances before concluding that she is right to pursue her revenge, even at the risk to Cinna's life. This decision is conveyed in Scene 2 to her confidante Fulvie, who questions the need for action since Auguste is bestowing favours daily on his adoptive daughter, and in any case other Romans, less personally involved, could get rid of the tyrant. Emilie is unmoved and is counter-attacking when Cinna arrives hot-foot from a meeting of the conspirators where he has, he claims, firmed up their support and given last-minute orders for the next day. At this moment Evandre enters with the message that Auguste wishes to see both Cinna and Maxime. Emilie immediately senses a betrayal of the conspiracy, although, faced with Cinna's calmer response, she comes round and hopes that her fears are groundless.

The first three scenes of Act I, prior to the sudden appearance of Evandre, have thus been devoted to presenting the basic circumstances and feelings on which the intrigue is going to be built. Here we find all the elements of the *exposition,* that part of a seventeenth-century play which, it was considered, should contain at least the seeds of all later action, with no major character or development being introduced unexpectedly later. How well has Corneille laid the foundation on which the success of his play will depend?

In many respects Act I of *Cinna* is a model of an early 1640s exposition, moving from a monologue to a dialogue between a principal character and her confidante, then to a scene introducing a third figure who, in his descriptions, brings in a number of other, non-appearing persons, and finally to the arrival of a messenger whose news causes initial consternation and then decision-taking. The build-up in character numbers gives the impression of a smooth unfolding of events which we need to know, yet the opening act is more than just a steady progression in time through a series of new statements. The main scene is the third one, in which Cinna reports to his lover on the latest state of the conspiracy. It is his busyness with the preparations elsewhere which explains why the play starts with two scenes involving Emilie, including the last opening soliloquy in French classical tragedy. As instigator of the conspiracy and its strongest member, Emilie is on an emotional high as the curtain rises: she has 'psyched herself up' for impending action, is now aware that her feelings are getting the better of her (ll.1-8), and stands back a little in order to think through the murder of her father Toranius, her attitude to Auguste, and the risks facing Cinna who, with others' help, will have to carry out the deed. For a moment (ll.35-40) she thinks of calling off the assassination, then her need for revenge gets the better of her (ll.41-52). While the second half of her soliloquy is thus a fairly rational examination of Cinna's position, Emilie is still in part controlled by vengeance (line 1) and grief (ll.3-

4), all summed up in 'ce bouillant mouvement' (line 19), the whirlpool of strong, instinctive feelings which she knows lie behind her desire. This mixture of human emotions is certainly quite different from the passive lamentations commonly found in tragedies of the 1630s and 1640s. Unlike many seventeenth-century dramatic monologues, Emilie's had ended with a clear decision (ll.53-57), giving Fulvie in Scene 2 a motive for trying to lower the temperature (line 62) and stress yet again the Emperor's benevolent side (ll.63-68). Implicitly accepting its existence (ll.69, 73, 77), Emilie sees herself as an outlaw's daughter whose role is to stir Rome up but in particular to exact personal revenge on Auguste. Fulvie's remarks on the danger to which Cinna will be exposed kindle new doubts in her mistress (ll.118-24), but her resolve is quickly restored: either Auguste will be killed, or Cinna will die, with her death to follow his (line 140).

The two-stage explanation of the link between personal motives and the apparently impersonal conspiracy has several advantages. Fulvie's counter-arguments force Emilie to further clarify and justify her own attitudes, and the two scenes give the audience a better chance than just one would afford to assimilate facts and emotions. Emilie now needs to have her determination tested by Cinna, who takes the main role in Scene 3. His uninterrupted harangue (ll.157-260) has been criticised as much too long, self-indulgent, and over-exuberant. It constitutes an excellent example of the *récit* by which dramatists provided eye-witness accounts of an event occurring off-stage which either could not or need not be shown live to the audience. Here, Corneille wants to show us a committed but essentially naïve Cinna, revelling in his organisational role but as yet untouched by the personal consequences. Hence the boyish enthusiasm and confidence with which Cinna recounts the state of play, restates his rallying-call, and details the crimes of Auguste which justify the conspiracy. What is in striking contrast to Scenes 1 and 2, however, is the absence of any mention of the real reason for the conspiracy, hinted at only in his opening and closing comments to Emilie herself (ll.152, 260). Rather he has been preaching the 'succès qu'on obtient contre la Tyrannie' (line 253), leading his fellow-conspirators to believe that the aim is 'le sort de Rome' (line 165), the final element in the dissolution of the second triumvirate of Lepidus, Mark Antony, and Octavian (as Augustus had become known after his adoption by Julius Caesar in 44 BC): 'Mais nous pouvons changer un Destin si funeste,/Puisque de trois Tyrans c'est le seul qui nous reste' (ll.221-22). The true motive will not become public knowledge until much later, and it is on this fundamental misunderstanding that Act II and part of Act III will be built.

The atmosphere of Scene 3, with Cinna oblivious to possible dangers and Emilie seemingly determined to put her earlier doubts behind her, concludes the setting-in-place of a mood of bustling optimism. The lyrical extravagance of Cinna's words and Emilie's final call to arms provide a deliberate contrast with the news brought in Scene 4. Auguste has commanded and must be obeyed, but time is short: indeed, Evandre has retained the imperial messenger Polyclète in order to give the conspirators a few extra moments to reflect. Interestingly, it is Emilie who cracks, suggesting that her private revenge be now abandoned and that Cinna take flight (ll.299-301). Her lover reminds her of his duty to 'la cause publique' (line 306) and to the other conspirators (line 309), and this firm response helps to strengthen Emilie's resolve once again.

Act I has thus conveyed much information, although most of it has come from the perspective of two characters whose primary motive is self-interest but who are successfully misleading Maxime and the other, unnumbered plotters into believing that the good of Rome is the sole aim. This clash between private and public will last throughout the play and provide one of the necessary dichotomies on which drama depends. It is articulated in the opening act through contrasting moods: Emilie's fears and determination in Scene 1, the arguments of Fulvie against hers in Scene 2, the excessive optimism of Cinna measured against Emilie's greater realism in Scene 3, and the steadfastness of Cinna overcoming Emilie's doubts in Scene 4. The tragedy will proceed through the constant, dynamic development of such opposing points of view. Imperceptibly to the reader, more obviously to the theatre audience, a blend of fact, opinion and emotion has been conveyed, arousing intense interest, raising questions, and leaving much detail still to be filled in. In retrospect, if not at the time, we note the passing references to Livie (ll.81, 346-48) and to the advisory role which Maxime and Cinna play at the Imperial Court (ll.294-95). Auguste has been physically absent, yet ever-present in the minds of all the speakers.

Within the 'historical' time-frame, only minutes elapse between Cinna's exit and his reappearance with Maxime in Auguste's audience chamber. Act II is unusual in seventeenth-century France in having but two scenes of greatly varying length, 290 and 62 lines respectively. This alone suggests a quite different purpose from that of Act I. There the *exposition* was completed at the end of Scene 3; the short Scene 4 had called in question many of the assumptions of the opening scenes; Act II will now reveal whether, as all fear, the conspiracy has been betrayed and, if so, what the consequences for them are.

Auguste's first action is to dismiss his courtiers and closet himself with Cinna and Maxime. To their astonishment, and to our great surprise too, the scene then develops, not into a denunciation but into a lengthy and in places philosophical argument on the merits and drawbacks of Empire compared to a Republic, and specifically on the wisdom or otherwise of Auguste retaining power. Each of the three men has his say: Auguste in three speeches (eighty lines in all), Maxime in four (seventy-nine lines), Cinna – perhaps predictably – in five, totalling 133 lines. Within this division, an initial section allows Auguste to explain his basic position, then Cinna and Maxime put forward theirs. The second half of the scene consists of generally shorter statements conveying the give-and-take of genuine, at times impassioned argument before the Emperor exercises his right to wind matters up.

What neither we nor the chief conspirators have expected is a world-worn Auguste seeking advice from his much younger counsellors on what to do with the burden of power. Yet, unlike less talented dramatists of his time, Corneille does not prolong unnecessarily the misunderstanding which has led Cinna and Maxime to fear the worst. Just as they had little chance to ponder their fate during the first interval, so now Auguste soon comes to his point. Quite unaware as yet of any threat, he has been turning his thoughts for some time to the transient nature of his position, the absence of peace of mind, the conflicting examples provided by immediate predecessors such as Sulla, a dictator who had abdicated and survived in the short term, and Julius Caesar, who retained power only to be assassinated. To their amazement, Cinna and Maxime are then invited, as friends, to give frank advice (ll.399-400).

Auguste's opening remarks barely give Cinna time to assimilate what he has heard. He needs a further few moments (ll.405-12) to fully gather his thoughts. What follows is a passionate defence, not of Republican government but of the Imperial status quo, a justification of Rome's conquest and a ringing endorsement of Auguste's personal actions. His final comment, that he is sure Maxime will support his remarks, forces the latter to concede the legitimacy of Auguste's rule, but he overcomes his shock at Cinna's apparent change of heart and launches into a two-part argument, initially defending the Emperor's right to choose, to demonstrate his strength of will (*vertu*) by following what his instincts dictate (ll.451-80), then moving from the private to a more public area, that of what Rome desires – which is certainly not an Empire resembling the despised rule of kings.

These initial statements give way to a less guarded political debate (from line 499), with Cinna arguing for the stabilising presence of 'un bon Prince' (line 504), firm but fair, as against less orderly rule by the people, Auguste reminding him of Rome's hatred of kings, and Maxime agreeing that popular government is what Romans now want, even if other countries prefer different systems. In a second stage (ll.545-620) the gloves come off between Cinna and Maxime, with Rome's various earlier experiences being put forward as examples to follow but with Cinna stressing the risks of excessive freedom which fosters jealousies and civil war rather than unity and stability. After a final appeal to Auguste to consider Rome's interests rather than his own, the Emperor gives his decision (ll.621-46), heeding Cinna's call for pity by agreeing to retain power, but sharing it by making Maxime Governor of Sicily and giving Emilie in marriage to Cinna.

This sustained scene has been one of consultation, exploring the political alternatives facing the Emperor and Rome, and apparently bringing to an end a long period of self-doubt for Auguste. But it does more than that. Its benevolent tone, Auguste's rapid if reluctant acceptance of Cinna's views while acknowledging the validity of Maxime's, and his rewarding of his two advisers all serve to paint a totally different picture from that which was given to us in Act I. It is to Cinna's and Maxime's credit that neither betrays excessive surprise, which could have been their undoing. But a further disparity lies in the difference between Maxime's honest explanations and the self-serving hypocrisy of Cinna: the latter ironically uses talk of the ever-present threat of assassination as an argument for maintaining the position of the man he has agreed to kill but who must die, while still Emperor, by his hand. Audience and conspirators are astonished by the new and patently genuine face of Auguste, but in addition Maxime is bewildered by Cinna's political stance. Scene 2 is therefore designed to bring clarification, and in particular reassurance to Maxime. Again Cinna is the more loquacious, quick to focus on what he knows is the only way to get out of a tight corner. Auguste's show of repentance is no substitute for revenge, he claims; the evil of Empire has to be uprooted, strength of purpose must predominate over the *amabilité* which Maxime preaches. He, Cinna, will accept Emilie nonetheless, but only after Auguste's assassination. The discussion ends with Maxime's surprise that Emilie might wish a husband in such circumstances, 'teint du sang de celui qu'elle aime comme un père' (line 702). Without in any way revealing his true motives, Cinna has thus succeeded in placating his fellow-conspirator. What he has simply not had time to do is to reflect on the very different Auguste who has just spoken to them, and this will occupy him during the second interval and the opening moments of Act III, before he returns to the stage. In turn, Maxime needs to consider both the political implications and how Auguste's gift of Emilie affects his personal plans.

Acts I and II have been predicated on oppositions: Empire versus Republic, private versus public, but also the constant contrast between openness and secrecy, awareness and lack of awareness. The intimate connection between the love-affair, Emilie's revenge, and the conspiracy is known only to Evandre and to Fulvie (line 345); indeed Maxime has just been shown to be ignorant of Cinna's long-standing love (ll.701-03) and so far has refrained from disclosing his own interest in Emilie. These carefully constructed patterns of suppressed or only partially revealed knowledge are overturned between the second and third acts. The impetus given to the intrigue at this point demonstrates the vital part played by intervals within a play. They can be dead times, but a talented dramatist will use them to advance the action through events which need not occur on stage. Without repeating information from Act I, Corneille has Cinna tell all to Maxime (ll.709-12), just as after the third interval we will come in on only the very tail-end of Euphorbe's account to Auguste (line 1077), the detail having been shown to us in Act III, Scene 1. In each case, the information results in a radical change of atmosphere. As the members of each side of the conspiracy are enlightened, the two sides will come together, first when Maxime discloses his love to Emilie in Act IV, Scene 5, then in the short series of meetings between Auguste and the conspirators in Act V.

Of the three freedmen or confidants included in the cast-list, Euphorbe is by far the most developed. In Act III, Scene 1 his role as adviser only becomes important because his master Maxime quickly reveals that he is Cinna's rival for the 'beaux yeux' of Emilie (line 771), yet in a quandary about how to win her affections. Maxime sees that Euphorbe's suggestion of betraying the conspiracy would prevent her personal revenge on Auguste from being realised, thus making him no more acceptable to her as a potential lover than he thought Cinna would be, coming as a gift from Auguste. Although correct in stressing Cinna's self-interest (ll.745-46) and possible fickleness (ll.753-56), Euphorbe has no ready answer to Maxime's predicament (ll.781, 791). A decision is delayed until after Maxime has seen how the land lies with Cinna.

The Cinna who appears in Scene 2 and whose plight will dominate the rest of Act III has had some time to reflect and has come to realise the conflict between his love of, and promise to, Emilie and the Emperor's unexpected benevolence. Now filled with remorse (ll.803, 832), he in turn can find little to counter Maxime's strongly ironical accusations of treachery, weakness, and short-sightedness. If both men are heavily compromised, it is, logically, from the effective leader of the plot that the next move must come. The antitheses contained in his comments to Maxime (ll.797-98, 817) and his description of himself as on the verge of anguished despair (line 858) indicate the need for the sort of self-examination which only a soliloquy can provide. The crucial monologue of Scene 3, a little shorter than Emilie's, is also very different in its form, moving from indecisiveness to a stage of apparent decision-taking, only to end with the realisation that he is wholly dependent on his lover, her hatred of the Emperor, and her memory of her father Toranius. Thus Cinna's instinctive respect for Auguste (line 881) and his gratitude for what he has been offered cannot overcome the commitment he has given to Emilie: 'Ma foi, mon cœur, mon bras, tout vous est engagé' (line 895).

Emilie has not been seen since the end of Act I, when she went off to use whatever influence she might have with the Emperor's wife. In the event, that had proved unnecessary, for Auguste had told both women the outcome of the deliberation (ll.908-10). Confident that her earlier fears were misplaced, Emilie now confronts a despairing Cinna (Scene 4), substantially weakened by his own arguments in the previous scene and seemingly unable to take any initiative. The meeting forms the literal but also emotional centrepiece of the play, the turning-point in the action. Either the assassination attempt will be dropped in favour of acceptance of the new Auguste's power-sharing proposals or, despite these concessions, the purely self-interested motives of Emilie will prevail. In what is the second-longest scene of the play, Emilie's strong personality and relentless pursuit of her limited aims gradually grind down Cinna's resistance. As Maxime has just done, she accuses him of feeling remorse (line 932), of lacking steadfastness, whereas she claims to be consistent with her aims (line 914), unassailable by Auguste (line 943). Compared to Cinna's 'slavish' attitude to the Emperor (ll.981, 1032) and his support of 'tyranny' (line 1013), the former's claims to have resisted the abdication for her sake cut little ice with Emilie. She will simply take her custom elsewhere and deny him the pleasure of being worthy of her (ll.1027-28). But – and it is an important concession as well as a threat – her love is still there, for him and for no-one else (ll.1033, 1037), since Cinna's failure to act would result in her carrying out the assassination herself, even at the cost of her own life. It is this emotional blackmail which finally persuades an ever-so-reluctant Cinna to accede to her wishes, but with the promise of a conscience-saving, honour-protecting suicide to follow (ll.1062-66).

However, what gives much added interest to this climactic encounter is the short coda which follows the lover's emotion-charged 'Adieu' (line 1067). Emilie had declared her fearlessness at the start of Scene 4; when we next see her, with Fulvie in Act IV, Scene 4, she will still be confident (ll.1267-68) and will use this self-control to dismiss Maxime's advances out of hand (Act IV, Scene 5), while her final appearance in Act V, Scene 2 is one of defiant rebellion against Auguste. In just a few lines, though, at the end of Act III Emilie's femininity and vulnerability break through: she weeps and asks Fulvie to persuade Cinna to live on. Yet she cannot bring herself to call off the assassination either and, in a striking mirror-image of Cinna's attitude at the close of his monologue, she leaves it to him, after Auguste's death, to decide whether to live for her or take his own life. Despite Cinna's reluctant agreement, then, Act III, like Acts I and II, ends on a note of uncertainty, with the audience again poised for whatever developments occur before the next act begins.

Both leading male conspirators have come to a decision during Act III, Cinna under duress, Maxime as a result of his less than satisfactory interview with Cinna. Having weakly given in to Euphorbe's arguments, Maxime now decides, in the latter part of Act III, to play the hand suggested to him and betray his co-conspirator. His dignity and perhaps lack of courage dictate that the news is disclosed by an underling who, being Euphorbe and more than just a messenger, denounces Cinna in comprehensive fashion and then spins an unlikely tale about Maxime's repentance and suicide by drowning. Although aware of Emilie's role in the conspiracy, Euphorbe has not implicated her, as Auguste's reaction in Act IV, Scene I demonstrates (the 'Furie' of line 1097 is Cinna, not Emilie). But by greatly blackening his friend's character (ll.1089-94), he has shifted responsibility very effectively on to Cinna alone and allowed himself time to engineer the abduction of Emilie. It should be noted, though, that Auguste follows the report of Maxime's 'juste repentir' (line 1088) with an unconditional and immediate pardon (ll.1101-02): the story of Maxime's fatal jump by night into the Tiber sits uneasily alongside this initial, unexpected, magnanimous clemency, showing that Euphorbe is out of his depth when faced with unforeseen developments.

Unlike earlier acts, where there was one clear focus (the conspirators in Act I, Auguste in Act II, Cinna in Act III), Act IV is divided between two groupings: Auguste and his visitors, and Emilie and Maxime. In switching from one set of characters to the other after Scene 3, Corneille breaks a stage convention of the time that approved of changes of scene only between acts and not within them. The *Examen* which Corneille first published to accompany the 1660 edition of the play justifies this infringement by the impossibility of having conspiratorial discussions in a place which Auguste has just used to hear Euphorbe's revelations. Just as Cinna needed an opportunity to digest Auguste's new personality and Maxime Cinna's apparent betrayal of the conspirators' ideals, so Auguste requires time to come to terms with Euphorbe's news. With this information coming at the end of an interval and in the opening moments of an act, Corneille has to call on a different topic to fill the rest of his 350 lines. What better way to raise the profile of both Emilie and Cinna in preparation for Act V than to bring back the far-from-dead Maxime and have him comprehensively humiliated by Emilie? For the more united the chief conspirators appear politically and emotionally when they meet Auguste, the greater will be the impact of his clemency.

Thus the latter part of Act IV will anticipate the events of Act V. But so do the opening scenes, with Auguste's instinctive response to what he is informed is Maxime's remorse, followed by two important encounters: the Emperor discussing, as it were, with his present and former selves in a soliloquy (Scene 2), and his meeting with Livie (Scene 3). Auguste's monologue is unlike the first two we have seen in *Cinna*. His inner thoughts range widely, from initial despair at the news of the conspiracy (ll.1121-29), through consciousness of his own criminal past as Octave (ll.1130-44) and a conviction that the conspirators' treachery is therefore justified (ll.1145-48), to a realisation of Cinna's role in the affair (ll.1149-58) and a rejection of thoughts of pardon (ll.1159-61), then on to a horror of further bloodshed (ll.1162-68) and to thoughts of suicide which would meet Rome's call (ll.1169-79), ending with a desire to see Cinna punished, by his witnessing his (Auguste's) death (ll.1180-85) or – on second thoughts – by having the conspirator killed first (ll.1185-86). Like Cinna, he cannot decide between living and dying, but then has the good fortune to receive a visit from his wife.

Enlightened by Euphorbe (line 1195), Livie advocates a change of tack, a pardon which would disorientate Cinna, be politically advantageous to Auguste, and yet have a chance of calming Rome. Auguste, however, would prefer abdication (ll.1221-28) and the peace of mind it brings, otherwise death (line 1236), and in the face of his wife's objections he gives her a short, sharp lesson on his experience of power (ll.1247-54) before exiting abruptly, leaving her with the hope that she may still be able to bring him to his senses (ll.1263-66).

Thus ends what had become a heated disagreement, requiring a cooling-off period but hinting at the possibility that the situation can be retrieved. Emilie's arrival in Scene 4 and her stated peace of mind (line 1268) is a change of scene, but also a studied contrast with the doubts and prickliness of the still shocked Auguste – and this despite the news which Emilie receives that Cinna, won over by Fulvie as instructed in Act III, Scene 5, had been on his way to see her when a sudden order made him divert to the palace. To add to Fulvie's fears are the rumoured arrests of Evandre and Euphorbe and unconfirmed reports of Maxime's drowning. This package of bad news, all understandable to an audience which, unlike any of the cast, has witnessed every scene of the play, leaves Emilie strangely unaffected, conscious only that her earlier fears and her present tranquillity defy logical explanation (ll.1293-96). This further contrast between principal character and confidante is in part a time-filler while Auguste gets ready to accuse Cinna, but the misplaced calm she feels also allows Emilie to dominate Maxime who now appears (Scene 5), warning that Evandre has confessed and that she herself is about to be arrested. But, ever resourceful, he and a fellow-conspirator have a handy skiff waiting in which she and he can make good their escape, returning later, of course, to avenge Cinna properly... This bizarrely romantic proposal from a direct-replacement lover (ll.1347-48) gets short shrift from a woman who says that his best hope is to deserve her tears (line 1360) and briskly leaves the amorous slave (line 1389) to his own devices.

Maxime, a figure of some importance nonetheless in the plot of *Cinna*, needs to have his say. In the last and least edifying of the monologues (Scene 6), he wallows in fear and self-pity, conscious of betraying Emperor, friend and 'mistress' with nothing to show for it all. He turns the slave epithet on Euphorbe, pinning the blame for his plight on the latter's base advice which got the better of his own more honourable nature and looking forward to his salvation, guaranteed by shedding the freedman's blood.

Scene 6 constitutes the culmination of the *nœud*, the complication of the plot which arose from the earlier *exposition*. A final act will contain the dénouement, the form of which is not yet clear, although the play's early subtitle *la Clémence d'Auguste* indicates *what* will happen, if not how or exactly when. In the middle of Act IV Livie had shown a desire to see her husband again, yet there will be no textual evidence in Act V that such a meeting has taken place. The Auguste we find in Scene 1 of the last act is, it would seem, simply the product of time and reflection which has changed him back into a rational, decisive leader, interrogating the person who he believes is the sole surviving leader of the conspiracy. Closely following Seneca's account, Corneille shows the Emperor briskly putting Cinna in his place, stressing the family's long hostility towards him, paradoxically rewarded, in Cinna's case, with gifts and honours, making him a trusted adviser, and giving him Emilie's hand in marriage (ll.1435-76). A second stage in the accusation (ll.1482-96) details the arrangements for the assassination, devastating proof of the extent of his information. Unable to fathom why Cinna rejected the offer of abdication in Act II, Auguste damns the conspirator with faint praise (ll.1518-22), reminding him of his absolute dependence on his influence and protection. Initially speechless (line 1541), Cinna assumes sole responsibility for his crime, planned, he says, as legitimate revenge for the assassination of his grandfather Pompey in 48 BC and the subsequent killing of Pompey's two sons (ll.1546-49), and defiantly asks for death. Emilie's arrival (Scene 2), the boast that her love for Cinna was as nothing compared to the revenge killing she in turn sought from him, and her pleading for death alongside Cinna make Auguste distraught. Livie, who had accompanied Emilie, intervenes to draw a distinction between, on the one hand, the former Octave and the legitimacy of State killings and, on the other, the present Emperor (ll.1605-16). Still in despair, Auguste lets Cinna and Emilie vie, in a short contest of wills, for the title of instigator of the conspiracy (ll.1619-56), with their agreeing in the end to share both the responsibility and the inevitable punishment.

In a way, each of these two characters has ended *en beauté* – undone, defeated, yet proudly defiant. However the third and last arrival, Maxime, although seemingly the trigger for the great clemency which takes even Auguste unawares, remains at the lower level where his recent behaviour has placed him: confessing his guilt, assuming responsibility, explaining his planned abduction of Emilie, seeking death but, as in his soliloquy, laying much of the blame on Euphorbe. The general pardon, the terms and meaning of which we shall look at elsewhere, is followed by acceptance speeches from Emilie, Cinna and Maxime and a final intervention by Livie, prophesying a long, glorious and conspiracy-free reign for the 'maître des cœurs' (line 1764) and a seat for him amid the immortals.

In three *Discours* or treatises on drama which he published in 1660 along with individual *Examens* or analyses of *Cinna* and his other plays, Corneille provides important comment on aspects of our tragedy's structure. Following Aristotle who advocated plots of suitable length and completeness, Corneille writes in the *Discours du poème dramatique*: 'Il faut donc qu'une action pour être d'une juste grandeur ait un commencement, un milieu, et une fin. Cinna conspire contre Auguste, et rend compte de sa conspiration à Emilie, voilà le commencement; Maxime en fait avertir Auguste, voilà le milieu; Auguste lui pardonne, voilà la fin' (*1*, III, p.128). This apparently facile outline brings out very clearly the focus on two matters: the conspiracy and the clemency. Earlier in the same *Discours* comes the comment that the assassination plans, the betrayal of them, and the arrest of Cinna are not sufficient in themselves; the audience needs to have its mind put at rest concerning what happens to the accused (*1*, III, p.125). These examples highlight Corneille's professional concern for a clear but well-rounded plot, with the subject-matter kept in proportion at all times, and a distinction made between main and subsidiary items. For him, the consultation scene, Cinna's remorse, his debate with Emilie, and Maxime's attempted seduction of her are *épisodes*, necessary steps in the plot but of secondary importance compared to main events such as the betrayal of the conspiracy, Auguste's despair, and Livie's advice. Love and politics (or love and revenge disguised as politics) constitute the themes of *Cinna,* but it is important to recognise that in 1642 Corneille follows his normal practice of subordinating love to other ideals: the *Discours du poème dramatique* declares that, for him at least, the dignity of tragedy normally requires 'quelque grand intérêt d'Etat, ou quelque passion plus noble et plus mâle que l'amour, telles que sont l'ambition ou la vengeance; et veut donner à craindre des malheurs plus grands, que la perte d'une maîtresse [= 'attractive woman']' (*1*, III, p.124). The loss of such a person may be a less suitable topic for tragedy than matters of State, yet love should be included, since it pleases the audience. It can be the spring of the action, but not the main focus, which should be one or more other passions (note the term) such as ambition or revenge.

But Corneille is conscious of the need, not just to lay out his themes but to construct a framework of acts and scenes which maintain our lively interest. He prides himself, in the same first *Discours,* on having brought together the strictly unrelated matters of the conspiracy and the Emperor's consultation, allowing each to affect the other and, in turn, lead to later actions such as Maxime's betrayal. 'Cela suffit pour faire une surprise très agréable' (*1,* III, p.137), yet the unexpectedness of Auguste's deliberation depends for its effect on his having summoned Cinna and Maxime before the end of Act I and on our knowing that Maxime was among the plot-leaders. One could add that, although the shock caused by the benevolence of Auguste in Act II might seem reduced by Cinna's statement in Act I that he and Maxime were frequently consulted by the Emperor, the effect is fully maintained, firstly by Emilie's scornful dismissal of this bit of self-deception and then by the way the Emperor keeps the idea of assassination and punishment alive even as he explains his desires to the two advisers. This is where *Cinna* is such a major advance on even recent conspiracy tragedies in which the two sides – murderers and victim – are seen in parallel but never interact. We could expect this more static format in late Renaissance drama, but the same unimaginative separation is still evident in Scudéry's *La Mort de César,* played less than eight years before *Cinna.* There, Brute and Cassie, conspiring against César, are contrasted with Antoine and Lépide, counsellors and true friends of the dictator. The two factions do not meet until Act IV, Scene 2, and César is assassinated in the last scene of the same act. In Corneille's tragedy, on the other hand, the role of Auguste's counsellors is combined with that of Cinna and Maxime as conspirators. Thus not only is the cast-list of *Cinna* shorter; more importantly, conflicting motives and emotions are set up, and these arouse far greater audience interest than the simple, predictable attitudes of Scudéry's cast.

As we have seen, *Cinna* takes a story at its crisis and handles it in what is virtually 'real' time, where the events depicted last little longer than the performance. This success in creating what is the ultimate suspension of disbelief is given as an example by Corneille

in his third *Discours* (*1*, III, p.184). And yet, as he states there, the
compression of events has been achieved without tedious accounts of
prior or off-stage happenings. For example, Cinna's recounting to
Emilie in Act I of his exhortations to the conspirators is not factual
but a source of pleasure, 'un ornement qui chatouille l'esprit des
spectateurs' (*1*, III, p.179). In the *Examen* to the play he uses a
similar contrast, between the 'ornements de Rhétorique dont j'ai
tâché de l'enrichir' and the need to provide information in what he
concedes is a long, unbroken account (*1*, I, p.911). In fact Cinna's
words are both of these things – a source of essential details but
couched in pleasing, realistic terms. That Cinna is conspiring is clear
to us from Emilie's words before he arrives on stage; what interests
Corneille is to expand on the bare details, but to show at the same
time the psychological *effect* which they have on two very different
personalities. Similarly the soliloquies, and in particular the first, go
well beyond a mere recital of events. Emilie's monologue, the first
Discours tells us, 'fait assez connaître qu'Auguste a fait mourir son
père, et que pour venger sa mort elle engage son amant à conspirer
contre lui; mais c'est par le trouble et la crainte que le péril où elle
expose Cinna jette dans son âme, que nous en avons la connaissance'
(*1*, III, pp.137-38). At the end of the play, too, the dramatist has tried
to avoid artificiality, in particular an unnatural speeding up of
arrivals and an excessive number of scenes.

All this underlines the skill with which Corneille has taken two
known historical events – Cinna's conspiracy and Augustus's
clemency – and expanded what was unexplained into a sequence of
scenes and acts which focus on a few hours in the present but blend
in information from the past and, at the end, open up a vista of the
future. The invention of Emilie as motivating force and the creation
of Maxime as both conspirator and unrequited lover provide
opportunities for memorable encounters but also for mis-
understandings or blissful ignorance based on inadequate or
deliberately delayed information. Although there is much more to
Cornelian tragedy than the creation of surprise, uncertainty and
suspense are key devices by which the playwright maintains the
momentum set in place by linking of scenes within each act. Thus at

the end of Act I we, like the stage-characters, wonder what will be the outcome of Auguste's summons. Act II leaves us unsure of Cinna's plans, while Act III closes with Emilie's emotional breakdown. Even the last scene of Act IV foresees Emilie's death on a (highly anachronistic) scaffold and Maxime's humiliation – a very different outcome from the one which will materialise shortly afterwards. The questions and doubts which remain in our mind each time the stage empties carry the action forward relentlessly, ensuring the maintenance of tension and giving the characters little time for second thoughts.

2. The Play in Performance

As far as we can tell from tantalisingly incomplete evidence, the Théâtre du Marais had six actors and three actresses on its books in the summer of 1642. Of the thirteen performers signed up the previous year, six were forcibly transferred at Easter 1642, on the King's orders, to the rival Paris troupe, the Hôtel de Bourgogne, which was languishing with only two actors and three actresses. The remaining five actors and two actresses would have reduced the Marais complement to its lowest level since its foundation in 1634. In 1644 there are two confirmed additions to these seven, resulting in six male and three female members, and given that both *Cinna* and its successor *Polyeucte* call for casts of nine, it is possible that the new recruits were in fact taken on two years earlier. One of the company, Julien Bedeau known as Jodelet, was unsuitable for playing tragedy, excelling rather in stock, farcical roles. Yet his absence from *Cinna* could be covered, since Evandre and Polyclète, very minor parts, are never on stage together and may have been played by the same actor.

The staging of *Cinna* raises two, quite separate issues: how was the play performed originally? And how might it be performed today? The latter question is open to multiple answers, given the variety of theatre designs, staging techniques and audience types available now. The more interesting matter, and not just for historical reasons, is: what stage system did Corneille have in mind when he gave his script to the Marais? It so happens that the early 1640s was precisely the time when French theatre companies were moving from a medieval multiple set (the so-called *décor simultané*) to – or towards – something very different, the single set or *décor unique* (sometimes called the *palais à volonté*).

In the multiple set, a number of different places were shown simultaneously, represented by small, curtained areas or compartments arranged round the three walled sides of the stage. While some of these compartments or *mansions* might be practicable, most could not be used for action. The actual location of any one scene or act would be indicated by the actors and actresses emerging from the appropriate compartment and performing in the centre or at the front of the stage, their position in that neutral no-man's land being then assumed to relate to that represented by the compartment in question. Settings not in use had their small curtains (*tapisseries*) closed. Some indication of general place could be given by a painted stage backcloth, while the individual *tapisseries* might indicate more specific areas.

Obviously this type of stage set, conveying in largely symbolic fashion a range of not necessarily adjacent locations, paid little heed to the unity of place. It was increasing interest in this and in the other two unities of time and action during the 1630s which brought about a switch to a radically different system. But another factor was important in the change, too: the introduction of a front stage curtain (*rideau*). Our limited knowledge indicates that seventeenth-century technology, in particular the need for an efficient system of counterweights, did not allow a large, heavy curtain to be raised and lowered easily. For this reason, once introduced, it only went up just before the start of a play and came down at the end. As a consequence, the stage remained visible at all other times, making it difficult to change the sets in the course of a performance.

Writing in the late 1650s when a stage curtain certainly existed but referring also to performances of *Cinna* from earlier years, Corneille states in his third *Discours* (*1*, III, p.181) that the departure of characters from the stage had to be properly timed and motivated, but that their arrival – Emilie's in Act I, for example – could be handled more flexibly: the audience is expecting an entrance, which can only happen when the actor or actress emerges from behind the *tapisserie* (note this reference to a feature of the multiple set). This might suggest that no curtain went up at the beginning of a performance, including the first ones, but equally the statement is not incompatible with the existence and use of a stage curtain, together with some form of primitive proscenium arch which would have helped its smooth functioning.

It was discussion of the unity of time which made contemporaries of the early Corneille interested in the unity of place – logically enough, since a restricted timespan for the action of a play would seem to call for a limited number of locations which could be visited during that period. Gradually, place came to be seen, not as widely separated areas or even countries, but as neighbouring towns or regions, or sites within a single city, although not strictly contiguous. Thus Scudéry's tragedy *La Mort de César* (1635) calls for a minimum of three different settings: a public square, the Senate chamber, and the bedroom of César and Calphurnie. Only two years later Corneille's *Le Cid* contains, as its author says in the *Examen*, a rather bewildering number of places: 'tantôt c'est le Palais du Roi, tantôt l'Appartement de l'Infante, tantôt la maison de Chimène, et tantôt une rue ou Place publique' (*1*, I, p.705).

The criticisms which gave rise to Corneille's comments no doubt contributed to his next play, *Horace* (1640), being the first major French tragedy to have a strictly unified setting. 'La Scène est à Rome dans une salle de la maison d'Horace', we are told, and later in the century, when the play was performed at the Hôtel de Bourgogne, the set designer says: 'Théâtre [= stage set] est un palais à volonté. Au cinquième acte un fauteuil.' Unlike *Cinna*, *Horace* contains a representative battle; this is, of course, conducted off-stage and is handled by the device of having reports, including a mistaken one, brought back to the single location from the battlefield. Both *Polyeucte,* played in the early months of 1643, and *La Mort de Pompée,* performed later that year, comply with strict unity of place. In what setting was *Cinna* first performed?

In *La Pratique du théâtre,* the abbé d'Aubignac writes: 'Je n'ai jamais pu bien concevoir comment M. Corneille peut faire qu'en un même lieu Cinna conte à Emilie tout l'ordre et toutes les circonstances d'une grande conspiration contre Auguste, et qu'Auguste y tienne un conseil de confidence avec ses deux favoris.' Is it 'un lieu public' or 'un lieu particulier' (Livre IV, chap. 3; *6*, pp.302-03)? The critic is not quibbling about dual use as such being made of a single location, but about the particular nature of *Cinna* as a conspiracy tragedy and the *invraisemblance* of one place, apparently open to many people, being used for plotting at all, far less for sharing with the intended victim. Conscious of the problem, Corneille responds in the 1660 *Examen* to the play: while the whole action takes place within Rome and quite conceivably within the Imperial palace precincts, the specific unity is breached by 'une duplicité de lieu particulier. La moitié de la Pièce se passe chez Emilie, et l'autre dans le cabinet d'Auguste' (*1*, I, p.911). It would have been quite absurd, he says, to have had fewer than two locations; hence the break in the *liaison des scènes* in Act IV. Critics are still divided on what exactly comments like these mean. Some, such as Georges Forestier (*5*, p.144) argue that the *liaison* break means that only one room in the palace was used, each of the two factions making it in turn their identifiable space. Others, including Georges Couton (*1*, I, pp.1575-80), argue that Corneille's words clearly suggest that there were two. Since this appears more plausible, the conclusion must be that, unlike the earlier *Horace* and probably the slightly later *Polyeucte, Cinna* may well have been originally played in a compartmented set consisting of two locations.

It was in the second half of the seventeenth century, by which time unity of place had become almost invariable practice, that dramatists could use the physical setting to good purpose, to explain or reinforce characters' moods and tragic dilemmas. Racine's *Bérénice* (1670) will be set within the Roman Emperor Titus's palace, in an antichamber strategically placed between his apartment and that of the woman he loves but is forbidden to marry, the Jewish queen Bérénice. Phèdre, the tragic victim in Racine's 1677 play of that name, fears that the walls and vaulted ceiling of the room in which the action takes place 'Vont prendre la parole, et prêts à m'accuser,/Attendent mon époux pour le désabuser'. Strict unity of place, then, can enhance the feeling of oppression, of claustrophobia, of impossible escape. By contrast, a *décor simultané*, even one representing only two rooms, cannot easily produce the same effect, and Corneille's *Cinna* does not seek to exploit a strong sense of location. Yet the very absence of this was one way of getting round the unity restriction and using the imagination of each spectator to invest the playing area with a more personal idea of physical setting. On the other hand, the single set or *palais à volonté*, taking on various attributes assigned to it by the playwright or director, was used later when *Cinna* was put on at the Hôtel de Bourgogne: props there consisted of an armchair and two stools in Act II (for the Emperor and his advisers respectively), then for Act V, Scene 1 an armchair for Auguste and a stool for Cinna, to his left rather than right to indicate the conspirator's subservience at that point.

In 1947 the director Charles Dullin presented a version of the multiple set in performances of *Cinna* staged at the Théâtre Sarah Bernhardt. He required four 'lieux scéniques', two of which were major locations: the 'chambre d'Emilie' and a 'salle dans le palais [d'Auguste]'. The latter was 'flanquée côté cour [= stage left, i.e. on the right as seen by the audience] d'une galerie intérieure'. Between the two main locations was 'une longue galerie qui divise les appartements, les éloigne aux yeux du spectateur et permet de donner toute leur valeur aux entrées et sorties des personnages'. As well as providing an exit route, this central stepped passageway gave access to the neutral fore-stage area (*proscenium*) and to the two *mansions* and could be linked through lighting to one or other of these main rooms. Dullin goes on:

> ...il convient que, lorsque l'action se passe dans la chambre d'Emilie, la salle du trône soit plongée dans la pénombre et *vice-versa*; quand l'action se passe dans cette salle, la chambre d'Emilie ne doit plus compter. Le couloir qui sépare les deux mansions doit être éclairé de façon à pouvoir desservir l'une et l'autre à tour de rôle; il doit donner de la profondeur au décor et, pour cela, sera traversé d'au moins deux traînées lumineuses qui éclaireront en même temps, au passage, les visages des personnages. (*3*, p.37)

The first three scenes of Act III were played in the stepped *galerie* and on the *proscenium* rather than in Emilie's apartment, with Scenes 4 and 5 being set, as the action dictates, *chez Emilie*. The *duplicité de lieu* in Act IV offered no problem for, as Livie exited up the stairway, the lighting on her dimmed and Emilie's room then became the focal point of the last three scenes.

While the Dullin production offered an interesting reinterpretation of a multiple-set performance, it differed necessarily from what the Marais provided for its customers. Dullin's alternate lighting of the two main locations and use of light to give depth to the set and illuminate characters' faces were all features unavailable in 1642. The 1947 stage had an opening of twelve metres, half as broad again as the Marais stage. The central steps had the effect of visibly separating the apartments of Emilie and Auguste, a luxury probably absent from the Marais where we must assume that at least some spectators, seated on each side, impeded the action and where the shallow stage left little room for both a downstage area and shadowy depths.

Partly as a result of inherited theatrical tradition but in part also because of the sheer physical constraints placed on seventeenth-century productions, playwrights needed to pay more attention to what was said, and how, than to their characters' movements on stage, which were unavoidably constricted. While there is, of course, no direct evidence of how *Cinna* was performed, much of the dialogue must have been declaimed from the front of the stage, a method called for by the poor acoustics of the typical *jeu de paume* and the continual noisiness of the audience. Unlike Racine, who was skilled enough to train certain of his actors and actresses to enunciate their parts, Corneille was famous for his inability to read even his own verse intelligibly in public. However, as a product of his times and in particular as a former pupil of the Jesuit college in Rouen, he was well trained in the techniques of formal rhetoric. In order to persuade his listener – and this was his prime duty – an orator had to consider in turn five parts or stages: the creation and development of arguments (*inventio*), their arrangement into a structured sequence (*dispositio*), the provision of embellishing figures of speech and other stylistic devices (*elocutio*), the role of memory in the delivery of speeches (*memoria*), and the importance of voice and gesture in what, even outside the theatre, was seen as a performance (*actio*).

Seventeenth-century French theorists of rhetoric largely followed the patterns first adopted by Aristotle, Cicero and Quintilian. The aim of a speaker was three-fold: to instruct his audience, to please, and to move. The orator should appeal to the intellect but also to the emotions of the listener. The second of the stages of oratory, *dispositio,* could be broken down into at least four sub-parts. An introduction to the topic under examination (*exordium*) was followed by a statement of the bare facts (*narratio*). This gave way to development of issues for discussion, arguments in support of a case and points against the opponent's case (*amplificatio*), and led eventually to a summary of matters raised and a conclusion (*peroratio*). The various stylistic features available to adorn the text and hold the audience included metaphor, metonymy, antithesis, periphrasis, hyperbole, anaphora, personification, apostrophe, and *sententiae* (the use of *sentences* or maxims).

As it happened, Corneille and his contemporaries in the theatre shared the general view of French imaginative writers of the time that literature should be both pleasurable and useful. *Plaire et instruire* was the guiding principle: how to entertain while at the same time ensuring that virtue triumphed and that evil was defeated. This double aim, at once aesthetic and didactic, fitted well with the precepts of formal rhetoric, and it is hardly surprising that Corneille above all, a trained although little-practising lawyer, should be conscious of rhetorical devices in composing his tragedies, in which there is typically the need for scenes of deliberation, scenes of judgement, and speeches designed to give praise or apportion blame.

An excellent example of a deliberative scene which adheres closely to rhetorical principles is Emilie's opening soliloquy. Its fifty-two lines divide fairly easily into four sections, starting with the introduction or *exordium* which sets the scene and above all the tone of this important self-analysis (ll.1-8). Then come the basic facts of the case (*narratio*): the death of her father and the nature of her dilemma, both contrasting with the apparent success of the killer (ll.9-16). The lengthy development or *amplificatio* (ll.17-44) can be subdivided into several stages: the dangers facing her lover (ll.17-24); possible outcomes (ll.25-34); her hesitations about allowing him to proceed (ll.35-40); her dismissal of these personal fears (ll.41-44). Finally, the *peroratio* (ll.45-52) contains her resolution to pursue her revenge and the assassination of Auguste.

This apparently clinical progression is, however, not quite what it appears. Although starting softly, Emilie works herself up to a high level of emotion, all the more impressive for coming so early in the action. The initial apostrophe, where she addresses her 'impatients désirs', extends to the end of the *narratio* (line 16) and is accompanied by a memorable personification, the 'désirs' being 'enfants impétueux', born like babies, then caught in the blind embrace of her 'douleur' (ll.1-4). The scene will end with a further, more extended personification involving her fears and her love (ll.45-52), and this gives the speech an added dimension, widening the argument to encompass Cinna, Auguste, her murdered father, and unnamed potential killers of her lover while at the same time concentrating on Emilie as the speaker and subject of the monologue.

Once the development stage of the scene is reached, Corneille introduces hyperbole (ll.16, 26), metaphor (ll.19, 32-34), metonymy (ll.24, 25), *sententiae* or moral maxims (ll.37-40), and a favourite device of his, antithesis (for example ll.18, 19, 27, 38, 48), all features which serve to heighten the tone of the presentation, to take the points made and examples offered to an extreme, to play on the gamut of feelings which Emilie has and which she wishes, as it were, to share with the audience. The *amplificatio* concludes with a series of what are in effect rhetorical questions (ll.41-44), contrasting with the softer line adopted after the exclamatory *Ah!* (line 35). The speech ends with imperatives ('Cessez', 'sers', 'montre-toi'), firmer than the 'souffrez que' of the opening (line 6).

The risk which Corneille took in beginning the play with a soliloquy was that Emilie would be seen to convey unrestrained emotion and little else. The result, however, is a carefully modulated and varied series of moods, largely concentrating on her self-absorption – half of the lines contain 'je', 'mon' or 'ma', while the ego is but barely disguised in the 'on' and 'notre'of lines 41-44. Yet the dangers which Cinna faces bring her out of her selfishness (ll.25-34), and the conclusion of her analysis is a determination to reconcile her passion and what she sees as her moral duty. Her former blind grief has been overcome, and now her love of Cinna, greater even than her hatred of the Emperor (line 18), can co-exist with her desire for illustrious revenge, although necessarily subservient to it. The passionate woman, self-justifying in her actions (line 17), is both rational and sensitive (line 5), fearful of the harm which her determination can inflict on her beloved, but firm, too, in her conclusions. Her self-examination allows her to take a decision from which she will not seriously deviate until after the clemency; it provides audience and reader with facts seen from a certain perspective, and above all it sets the tone of high energy and emotional involvement which will impel the progress of the play.

The remaining two scenes of the exposition offer similarities and differences. Act I, Scene 2, the meeting with Fulvie, adds only one fact to what we already know – Auguste's goodness towards his adoptive daughter – but it is a crucial piece of information, not denied by Emilie but ignored in her blind determination to avenge herself. Within the opening soliloquy a dialogue had, paradoxically, been engaged, as in her mind's eye Emilie addressed in turn her inmost urgings, then Cinna, then her fears and her love. Now it is conducted on a more conventional level, the confidante's potent argument contrasting with the self-satisfied pronouncements of her mistress, concerned as ever with herself but pretending to have Rome's interests at heart (ll.106, 108, 110) and elevating her thoughts to the level of general truths (ll.75-76, 83-84, 105-06, 130-32).

The final stage of the story-so-far (Act I, Scene 3) contains a comprehensive range of rhetorical devices, used by Cinna to embellish his account to Emilie of his meeting with the other conspirators. His main speech of one hundred and four lines is a fine example of successful persuasion. He has convinced the plotters as a group, and now he seeks to convince his lover as listener and, in a sense, himself as narrator, swept along, just as much as at the time of his original harangue, by abundant self-confidence tinged only with moments of doubt or modesty. As Corneille presents it, the speech combines first-person narrative and lengthy excerpts of direct speech, giving us a clear, vibrant impression of the recent event.

Many techniques are called into play in this breathless outpouring. Despite its apparent realism (Cinna has arrived hot-foot from the scene), his version of the off-stage encounter adopts the same four-part structural pattern as Emilie's monologue. Following an introduction (ll.163-72) comes the justifying list of the Emperor's crimes (ll.173-208, 215-20); the oration's development deals with the planned assassination (ll.221-36) before a brief summary/ conclusion (ll.237-40). This *récit* is preceded by a prologue for, as in the best dramatic accounts, the listener needs to be reassured from the outset, especially since Emilie had earlier mentioned the inherent dangers (line 142). Thus Cinna does two important things straightaway: he forecasts a happy outcome, so putting his beloved's mind at rest before the detailed account (ll.145-48), and he draws specific parallels between the commitment of the conspirators and both his service to Emilie and her personal vendetta (ll.149-52). Once his story is finished, he explains the effect it has had on his hearers (ll.241-48) and concludes with a personal address to Emilie (ll.249-60).

While reassuring the two characters on stage and the audience or reader, Scene 3 also broadens the picture in ways compatible with the limitations of the seventeenth-century stage. Corneille lets us imagine a range of supporting parts and of happenings beyond the few square metres of his playing area. This is one of the prime functions of Cinna's account, with its reference to 'cette troupe' (line 158) and his 'amis' (line 163), unnamed until, in Act V, Scene 1, Auguste gives a roll-call of the leaders among them (ll.1489-91). These non-appearing figures, essential in the mechanics of the conspiracy, come alive for us through Cinna's words. Wishing that she had been there to see for herself (line 157), he tells Emilie of their physical appearance, their outward reactions on hearing his words – he had seen their burning eyes, pale foreheads, and faces red with anger (ll.160-62) as, in turn, they moved through passion, fear and hate. As he had done to them, so to Emilie and us he presents verbal pictures (ll.177, 189), paintings (ll.189, 195, 206), using colours (line 193) and strokes (line 203) to depict Octave's victims and inflame his hearers. The second part of the *narratio* moves from the visual to the intellectual, tapping into the co-conspirators' mental processes as his words stir their minds (line 206) and produce in them rebellion ('impatience', line 209), agitation, and strong emotion ('frémissements', 'violence', line 210). This inner persuasion again produces outwardly visible effects (line 213) which encourage him to move to the climax of his presentation, the list of the Emperor's 'cruautés' and the arrangements for the assassination attempt.

The speech, the longest Corneille was ever to compose, can be no more than a summary: Cinna is out to convey essential detail but above all to create an impression on Emilie, and this he can only do through words. It makes little difference that his gallery of visual effects may be largely exaggerated: the impression he seeks to give is that of a commanding officer instilling last-minute bravado in his troops, and comforted by their instant, eager, unthinking reactions.

To convey this multi-layered performance, Corneille calls on many of the devices of oratory seen earlier: metaphor (in particular Auguste as the blood drunk tiger, line 168), personification (Rome with its entrails, line 178), and synecdoche or the part for the whole ('Aigle', line 179; 'fers', line 183; 'chaîne', line 184; 'joug', line 228). He makes use of anaphora or initial repetition ('jamais' in lines 145 and 147, 'Combien' in lines 169 and 170, 'Où' in lines 178 and 179), accumulation ('César', 'Auguste', 'Empereur', line 159; 'impie, affreuse, inexorable', line 190; violent deaths under the triumvirate, ll.197-202; the five atrocities introduced as 'Toutes ces cruautés', ll.215-18), exclamation (ll.169-72), and antithesis (ll.162, 171, 182, 186, and especially in his final address to Emilie, ll.250-60, couched in suitably melodramatic alternatives). His depiction of incidents is too specific and self-centred to allow for the generalities of *sententiae*, and events are too pressing, here as elsewhere in the play, for the luxury of periphrasis. The only time when embellishment is – appropriately – absent is in Cinna's recital of the assassination details (ll.229-36). The speech is a masterly combination of facts and emotions, of content necessary to us and to

Emilie, and of impressions made on his various listeners by his inflammatory, manipulative words and vivid verbal pictures.

It is instructive to compare Emilie's role at the beginning of Act I, Scene 3 with that of the conspirator Brute interrogating his fellow-plotter Cassie in Scudéry's *La Mort de César*. The purpose of both characters is the same, to seek information and dispel doubts, but the lightness of touch, the natural style and restraint of Emilie in questioning Cinna (ll.141-44) is very different from the ponderous, unvaried cross-examination by Brute:

> Enfin obtiendrons-nous le suprême bonheur?
> Voit-on en nos amis un sentiment d'honneur?
> As-tu bien observé les traits de leur visage?
> N'y remarques-tu rien de sinistre présage?
> Cette première ardeur est-elle dans leur sein?
> Ne succombent-ils point sous le faix du dessein?
> N'ont-ils point mis d'obstacle à leur gloire prochaine?
> Leurs esprits sont-ils joints par une même chaîne?
> Vont-ils d'un même pied? L'auras-tu bien pu voir?
> Et bref, qui règne en eux, ou la crainte, ou l'espoir?
>   (*La Mort de César*, II, 3, ll.381-90)

Emilie's two, apposite questions contrast forcibly with Brute's eleven and have the effect, absent in Scudéry, of drawing out from her interlocutor the lyrical account which both she and we, as audience or reader, require.

These three scenes, taken as a sample of Corneille's stylistic technique, not only create their own mood and raise the temperature to a level necessary early on in the play to grip the audience and retain its involvement; they also provide the required setting or background for subsequent events. The consultation scene (Act II, Scene 1) and Cinna's role within it would lose much of their power in the absence of Act I, Scene 3, with which it provides such a telling contrast. Similarly, without the delineation of Emilie as a decisive character (Act I, Scene 1) strengthened by her resistance to Fulvie's arguments (Act I, Scene 2), her reaction in Act I, Scene 4 and again in Act III, Scene 5 would have been weaker and could have undermined both her lover's and her own position in the following hours of the action. Corneille arouses the tragic emotions of pity, fear and wonder through contrast, one in which the audience is invited to compare the same characters but in different situations, for example in private and then in public, and to observe how successfully they deal with the clash of ideologies and loyalties which such stark juxtapositions produce. In the absence of a series of realistic settings and of almost all physical action, it is skill in such arrangement of conflicting situations which contributes to the stage success of a seventeenth-century tragedy.

A second example of the use of rhetorical devices in getting the message across the footlights might be Auguste's monologue in Act IV. The deliberation here is much more fraught than in Emilie's soliloquy; it ends not in decision but in anguished indecision, the Emperor attracted equally by suicide and by continuing power (line 1192). Within its seventy-two lines, however, it is possible to detect the same framework: an *exordium* (ll.1121-29), followed by a *narratio* (ll.1130-44), an extended *amplificatio* (ll.1145-86), and a *peroratio* (ll.1187-92). The structural processes contained in the finding of arguments (*inventio*) and their organisation (*dispositio*) and then the embellishment of the *elocutio* are designed to convey the heady mixture of anger and pity, thoughts of life and death which in turn assail Auguste. It is not surprising that, in these circumstances, exclamation features regularly (ll.1131, 1149, 1157, 1158, 1162), as do apostrophe (ll.1121-28),   the repetitions of anaphora (ll.1170, 1171, 1175, 1176, 1179), hyperbole (line 1166), metaphor (ll.1132, 1165-66, 1180), and the discomfort of generalised truths (the second *hémistiche* of lines 1129, 1160). The stageability of the scene is considerable, for this is a monologue which involves two speakers in one, Auguste and his alter ego Octave, a split personality struggling to come to terms with itself before it can tackle the problem posed by the conspiracy and its leader, Cinna.

While language, plain and adorned, seemingly natural in its crescendos and diminuendos, yet carefully planned and controlled, is a major part of the stage enactment, it would be quite wrong to think that practical constraints resulted in an absence of significant movement and gesture. Entrances and exits, combined with positioning in the playing area and the contrast between standing and sitting, speaking and listening, all contribute to the spectacle and to the audience's correlation of words and actions. Some of the evidence comes in specific instructions such as stage-directions or statements made by the author in critical writings, although most of it has to be gleaned from a careful study of the play-texts themselves.

Writers and publishers of seventeenth-century French tragedy were sparing with stage-directions, and *Cinna* has as few as any. Four of the five (following lines 356, 1099, 1262, and 1736) were added only late on, in the 1663 edition of Corneille's collected works. The fifth, following line 1102, was introduced in 1648, but until 1663 was placed after line 1100, illogically so since, before exiting, Polyclète needs to hear the message for Eraste contained in lines 1101-02. The four later stage-directions merely repeat what the dialogue at that point clearly indicates anyway, except for the final one, where Auguste addresses Cinna (line 1733), then both Cinna and Maxime (lines 1734-36) before turning to Maxime specifically (ll.1737-38) and then to all three conspirators (ll.1739-40) before returning to Maxime (line 1741).

It is from the text itself, though, that we must gather what we can about the physical props, the movements and gestures of characters, and other elements of staging. The actual print on the page can provide us with some important initial clues. The 1682 version of *Cinna*, the last overseen by Corneille and reproduced in most modern editions, contains fifty-five lines which begin with small indentations (see *4*), indicating each time a change of direction of some kind in the speech in question, a pause at least, very often a physical movement, a shifting of the speaker in his or her seat maybe, or even just an alteration in the character's gaze. In the absence of any Corneille play manuscript or contemporary actor's notes or annotated script, these indications offer valuable insight into how *Cinna* may have been played at the time.

The small break in the text can mark a simple switch in the argument, the adoption of a contrary point of view. 'Mais' is an obvious indicator of this in a few cases (ll.41, 893, 1149, 1162, 1545). In other places, it coincides with the end of self-questioning, a time of decision (e.g. ll.105 and 125). Cinna's report to Emilie in Act I is punctuated by breaks occurring with a change from first-person narrative to reported direct speech (line 163), or the start of a further argument (line 189), or the use of a rhetorical question (line 205), or the beginning of a summing-up (line 249). Farewells, accompanied by exhortations, are another feature (line 317). In the consultation scene, indentations occur when Auguste has dismissed the courtiers and is closeted with his advisers (line 357), when he moves from an account of his dilemma to a request for assistance (line 393), or later when he reaffirms his decision to retain power and then grants Cinna and Maxime their rewards (line 633). In the same scene Cinna pauses after his initial surprise and before launching into his first reply (line 413), or when he summarises his divergence from Maxime's views and then elaborates his own (line 505), or again when he puts Maxime in his place (line 571), when he finishes a denunciation of so-called Roman freedoms (line 589), and before he begins his final eloquent appeal to Auguste (line 605). Maxime pauses for similar reasons, to move into a substantive argument (line 451), to add a new point (line 481), or to switch from a particular case to a general principle (line 535).

These examples, taken mostly from the first two acts, could be extended to the last three. Every scene containing substantial speeches is involved, except Act III, Scene 2 between Cinna and Maxime. The breaks allow the actor or actress to draw breath, in a rather more definite manner than elsewhere where punctuation within and especially at the ends of lines was used not just to indicate the sense of the words but as a guide to diction, marking the stresses and rhythms of stage speech. Modern editors tend to put extra commas at line-ends or replace an original comma by a semi-colon – small matters, perhaps, but subtle and unnecessary changes to the generally fluid patterns of diction which Corneille seems to have wished the Marais company to observe.

Noticing and then interpreting the facial expressions and physical movements of characters is more difficult. In the single-set *palais à volonté* of later in the century but also in the original, perhaps multiple set of 1642, some minimal furniture was provided. The Hôtel de Bourgogne productions featured an armchair and stools. The frontispiece to the first edition of the play shows Auguste in the last scene, wearing a wreath of laurel on his head and seated on a fairly ornate canopied throne set on a small dais, with pillars and balustrades and helmeted soldiers in the background. Cinna is in a suppliant position, on bended knee, touching the Emperor whose left hand rests on his head. Emilie is to Cinna's right, while Maxime is in the process of kneeling down behind the couple. Although there is often little relationship between such engravings and the text they are supposed to illustrate, the scene here represented coincides closely with what we must imagine occurs in the closing lines of the play.

Stage props and costumes in Corneille's day were a mixture of the historically correct and the anachronistically modern. Although Augustus was not an emperor in the seventeenth-century sense of the word and will not have had a throne, throne-room or crown, these are what Auguste, like Louis XIII, enjoys. To indicate his authority he will be seated, at least most of the time, and it is as a mark of displeasure that, at the beginning of Act V, he makes Cinna sit, on a chair ('siège', line 1425), to listen to his accusations. References to sitting down in seventeenth-century tragedy are rare, suggesting that characters stood more than we might expect. A seated position could indicate fatigue or dejection as well as power, as in the case of Racine's Phèdre who, once seated, finds herself a prisoner of her conflicting emotions, unable to move. Cinna is in a not dissimilar situation, instructed not to speak until invited and expected to remain seated at the same time. Thus when he momentarily ignores the Emperor's injunction and begins an objection (ll.1477-78), he jumps up, automatically, actions matching words. He is ordered to resume his seat (line 1479) and retains it until urged to respond ('Parle, parle, il est temps', line 1541). At this point, he presumably takes the opportunity to rise, or perhaps he waits for a few moments until the indented line 1545, for what he has heard has rendered him initially 'stupide' (line 1541), i.e. thunderstruck. At times during his two long speeches, the Emperor may descend from his throne (which, being raised slightly above the floor, allows him symbolically to dominate Cinna) and come and tower directly over him, contrasting his freedom of movement with the impotence of the accused.

The arrival of Emilie, accompanied by Livie and Fulvie, makes Scene 2 more crowded. While the silent confidante and, for most of the time, Livie can remain in the background, each of the two conspirators seeks the limelight, with Emilie defying Auguste and then engaging in a contest of wills with Cinna. These two attitudes will dictate the movements and gestures, Emilie standing close to the Emperor, then close to Cinna, partners in opposition. Dullin (*3*, p.149) has them holding hands when solliciting union, in life or death (ll.1650-56). Cinna's chair is unused.

The final tableau has a different kind of movement. On entry, Maxime is invited to approach the throne (line 1665) but, confessing his guilt, can be expected to throw himself immediately on his knees, remaining there for at least the start of his main speech (ll.1670-72). It is likely that, as he approaches the moment of clemency, Auguste stands, but if he moves away, he regains his throne and sits down by the time that Emilie expresses her submission (line 1715). The three guilty but forgiven conspirators then throw themselves in gratitude at Auguste's feet.

We can extend this type of analysis to other scenes in the play. While much of the consultation scene will see the three characters seated, Cinna may be on his knees (line 606) when making his final, emotional plea to Auguste. It is likely that, to mark the end of the consulting process and the moment of decision, the Emperor stands (line 621). In her opening soliloquy Emilie may be seated on a chair or couch, whereas both she and Cinna are likely to convey their sudden anxiety by remaining standing throughout Act I, Scene 4. If the text itself and the stage-directions give few direct instructions, we must extrapolate from what there is and try to match actions to words and moods. For example, the normally self-controlled Emilie bursts into tears following Cinna's departure at the end of Act III, Scene 4 : her confidante, who tells us this (line 1070), will adopt a compassionate, protective attitude towards her mistress during this momentary emotional breakdown. Elsewhere in the play, bowed heads and averted eyes will indicate feelings of guilt or ingratitude or humiliation, direct gaze and physical closeness the attempt to engage in frank discussion with one's interlocutor, while frustration or despair or anger can be conveyed by distancing oneself from others on stage.

For Corneille and his contemporaries, speech was action. As the first *Discours* of 1660 puts it: 'les actions sont l'âme de la tragédie, où l'on ne doit parler qu'en agissant, et pour agir' (*1*, III, p.133). Just as action must accompany speech, so it is the language of the play which very largely conveys to an audience the action of the plot and the activeness of its various characters.

3. Conspirators

It would be much too simplistic to divide the cast of *Cinna* neatly into the good and the bad, since a feature of this play is that moral rectitude on the one hand and tragic error or ingrained evil on the other are not the sole motivating forces behind any of the characters. Those plotted against or victimised in other ways are all flawed, while more than sheer villainy explains the deeds of the conspirators.

Non-appearing accomplices include the ten named by Auguste (ll.1489-90) and others whom he considers not worth mentioning (line 1493). Are these plotters part of the 'illustre jeunesse' (line 1173), the young men of noble blood whetting their swords to kill the Emperor, as Seneca has Augustus say? How many of them fit Maxime's description of ardent Republicans, 'ceux qu'engage avec nous le seul bien du pays' (line 760)? Corneille has left the answers deliberately vague. Requiring a critical mass of schemers, and some names which Auguste can flourish, he has not wanted to move the spotlight off the three central characters and their mixed, sometimes confused motives. The contrast is clear between the role given to the associates here and earlier conspirators such as Salvidien, Lépide, Murène, Cépion, and Egnace (ll.1202-05), all recorded in Seneca, all executed, and used by Livie as reasons why her husband should now adopt a different tactic.

Of the three named conspirators with speaking parts, two were invented by Corneille, while the third, Cinna, had to be developed considerably from brief details given by historians.

Maxime

Maxime has never had a good press. This is because he is seen as gullible, secretive, vindictive, jealous, easily led, an embarrassingly inept suitor, and the centrepiece of an improbably melodramatic false suicide and an abduction plan. He is indeed all of these things, and not many second-rank characters could rise above that combination of defects. But he is also the sole conspirator of the three to have and maintain a consistent political line. This could be admirable, yet his doctrinaire idealism may well be judged inflexible, even blind.

His projected role in the assassination plans is important but secondary: he and others are to secure the entrances while Cinna will lead the group which surrounds and kills Auguste (ll.246-47). A much more essential function is defending the Republican cause in the consultation scene debate. Although speaking second and therefore having more time to adjust to the unexpected, Maxime is wrongfooted by Cinna, forced to concede that Auguste has been legitimised (ll.443-46). He then argues that Auguste, able to do as he will, should follow his inspiration, and that renunciation is a greater virtue than possession of power (ll.461-80). Secondly he maintains that Rome is anti-monarchy, that ten attempts on Auguste's life prove the risk an Emperor runs, and that assassination would damage the record he leaves behind (ll.481-98).

When the debate becomes more political, Maxime asserts that Rome will not change its preferences, however misguided (ll.526-34), and he brings in the theory of nations (*climats*): each country has a preferred political system, and 'le seul Consulat est bon pour les Romains' (line 544). Cinna counters this with an equally valid theory of periods. His argument is no more developed but it gives rise to personal tensions (ll.557-64) and an unfortunate reference by Maxime to Pompey, allowing Cinna to seize the initiative and launch into a long, impassioned speech which proves to be the last before Auguste decides. Maxime has done well not to reveal the conspiracy (ll.491-93), using the earlier plots against Auguste to argue that abdication would result in salvation. But in the end he is no match for Cinna's rhetorical powers and love of talking. As recompense for his advice Maxime is made Governor of Sicily, a seemingly generous political appointment, although no doubt seen by Cinna and others as an exile from the seat of power in Rome.

The limitations of Maxime's vision are apparent in the following scene. Without yet indicating his love of Emilie, Cinna makes clear his concern for the past, present and future of Rome and with fundamental change. Unfortunate events after Julius Caesar's assassination, especially Cassius's suicide and Brutus's death, need not repeat themselves. Maxime, on the other hand, sees things in much simpler, primary colours: 'Je veux voir Rome libre' (line 651, cf. ll.685-86).

His role in the betrayal of the conspiracy in and after Act III is considered in discussion of Euphorbe in the next chapter. Suffice it to say that Maxime bears most, if not full, responsibility for the action. In his second meeting with Cinna (Act III, Scene 2), he has the upper hand in one sense, able to cajole a now doubting friend into not wasting a second chance to rid Rome of its tyrant and using at times what may be irony (ll.819-21), normally a sign of domination. Yet again he fails to push his case, allowing himself to be fobbed off with Cinna's anguish (line 858) and yielding ground with inappropriate lovers' jargon (line 861), although this, too, could be seen as ironical.

His final part is the most demeaning of all: the encounter with Emilie in Act IV, Scene 5. In his two previous plays Corneille also depicted an *amoureux* or unrequited lover, in different circumstances but, as in *Cinna*, playing the card of passion late in the action. Don Sanche in *Le Cid* ends with his honour saved, while Valère in *Horace*, although getting short shrift from the arbitrator-king, is finally an honourable figure too. Why, therefore, does Corneille humiliate Maxime, who naïvely explains his false suicide (ll.1316-18), invites Emilie to flee with him on the pretext that they can return later and avenge Cinna, and then offers himself as a friend and as a slave, a substitute ardent lover, 'un autre Cinna' (line 1347)? Emilie upbraids him for his lack of dignity, weakness, and unwillingness to die for the cause, leaving the conspirator to indulge in a monologue of self-pity, recriminations, attacks on Euphorbe, and what he terms 'un remords inutile' (line 1406) which merely hints at his own suicide. Derek Watts argues that 'without the rebuff he receives in [Act IV, Scene 5], he is unlikely to have repented in Act V' (*4*, p.169). It is true that he must be forced to take the initiative and confess his multiple sins. But, compared to Don Sanche or Valère,

Maxime is made a figure of fun at the end of Act IV. Significantly, though, he regains much if not all of his dignity in Act V, where he provides a reason for his disappearance, confirms the rationale for Emilie's abduction, still seeks Euphorbe's death (less unacceptable to a seventeenth-century audience than to us), repeats the description of his actions as an 'artifice' (line 1685, cf. line 1394), and begs leave to die in an honourable suicide. Maxime has to sink low in order to provide Auguste with yet further reasons for punishing or not punishing the conspirators. At the same time, he must have just enough status and credibility for the Emperor to take the threat he poses seriously. It is to Maxime's credit that he seizes his chance, confesses in full, not knowing the outcome but fearing the worst, and is then given the opportunity through the clemency to restore his self-respect.

That being said, it remains true that he cuts a generally unimpressive figure. His political views are clear but simplistic, and his suggestion in Act II that Auguste should let his inspiration guide him and the future of the Empire (line 473) reveals a lack of insight into the Emperor's true state of mind at that point. If Maxime is one of the leading co-conspirators, what does this tell us about the others and about Cinna's judgement in choosing 'des hommes de courage' (line 154)? Maxime has a belief in friendship and its responsibilities (line 735), but this does not withstand the jealousy he feels. If he criticises Cinna's self-interest, he soon succumbs to the same temptation to put his own interests first, and his betrayal is all the more tawdry because he fails to understand Emilie and her attitude towards Auguste.

Cinna

In preparing his play, Corneille carefully deleted Seneca's phrase describing Cinna as dull-witted, *stolidi ingenii.* Yet if Maxime was subservient to Cinna, so the ringleader is but a servant of the instigator of the conspiracy, Emilie. Circumstances and language change, yet love of her is always top of his agenda, ahead of her revenge, with political freedom for Rome in third and last position (see ll.877-78, for example). If at times he expresses himself as a courtly lover or an early seventeenth-century *héros de roman* (ll.260, 321-22), this could be attributed to his relative youth and inexperience, although there is an element of blind worship and hence the fear of sacrilege in his attitude ('j'idolâtre Emilie', line 813; 'je deviens sacrilège', line 817). Like Rodrigue with Chimène, he must show himself worthy of her (ll.136, 1028); fulfilling her revenge is the only means to that end. Emilie might be expected to have a different order of priorities, but even she can say, again in a monologue and without apparent irony, that 'J'aime encor plus Cinna, que je ne hais Auguste' (line 18). Their passion has spawned a revenge plot which has as a prize for success Emilie's hand in marriage. At the dénouement Cinna will claim that assassination of Auguste had crossed his mind before he fell in love with Emilie (line 1628), but he confirms that 'l'offre de mon bras suivit celle du cœur' (line 1632).

We have noted in chapter 2 the oratorical performance Cinna puts on in Act I, Scene 3, and his self-control in Scene 4, despite his extreme fear (line 293). On the political front, he talks in the opening act of 'liberté' and 'libertés', but he neither attacks monarchy as such nor defends republicanism. In particular, Auguste is not criticised, since his twenty-year reign has been peaceful, although Cinna appears to condemn those who deposed the dictator Caesar. As a result of his comments here and later, critics are divided on what personal opinions Cinna has, if any. Some (e.g. C. Dullin, *3*, p.18 and S. Tiefenbrun, *47*, pp.189-93) believe he has Republican sympathies. Others, notably S. Doubrovsky (*16*, p.197), consider that he is a covert monarchist, that his defence of the Empire in Act II rings true, whereas his address to the conspirators was that of a mere demagogue. A third possibility, expressed by A. Stegmann (*44*, vol.II, p.586) and O. de Mourgues (*35*, pp.57-58) among others, is that he has no firm political stance or cannot reconcile two conflicting positions.

Certainly in the consultation scene he puts forward no general arguments in favour of monarchy. Rather he comments only on the outcome of stable government, on the current state of affairs, and on the need for a good leader, and some of his anti-republican points are at best defective. Indeed, here if not earlier, we may question his judgement, for he thinks of Auguste as remorseful yet innocent (line 414), which he is not; Maxime has a clearer picture (line 465). Later, Cinna defends the status quo by stressing the orderliness of society under an emperor (ll.505-08), compared to the imaginary freedom under a republic (line 502) and the chaos of rule by bad consuls (ll.513-20), although consular government can be effective (line 550).

Immediately after the scene with Auguste and again in Act III, Cinna does his best to explain to Maxime his apparently inconsistent behaviour. His first response is to state that full revenge for Rome is required, not mere contrition from Auguste: the evil of tyranny must be properly eradicated (ll.677-80). Later his explanations are more considered and answer much if not all of the criticism of those like Voltaire (9, vol.54, p.133) who failed to understand how the Emperor's 'bienfaits' did not elicit an instant change of heart during or just after the consultation. Cinna's argument, that one becomes fixated with an original intention and only feels remorse and repentance as time for the deed approaches (ll.822-32), has much validity, backed up as it is here with a promise to give the Romans all that they expect of him (ll.853-54).

The next two scenes, however, forming the climax of the role and the turning-point of the action, emphasise the emotional turmoil in which Cinna is caught up. The self-examination of Act III, Scene 3 brings out his indecisiveness. In the centre of the monologue, he can express wishes and ask rhetorical questions, but both at the beginning and again at the end his hesitations and apparent self-abasement (line 882) are manifest. 'Ce discours est d'un vil domestique', wrote Voltaire, 'et non pas d'un sénateur romain; il achève d'avilir son rôle qui était si mâle, si fier, si terrible au premier acte' (9, vol.54, p. 143). The problem lies in the strength of his love and what he has allowed that love to promise. Ironically, laws in the political sphere, whether benign (line 425) or tyrannical (line 670), have given way to even more binding and oppressive *lois de l'amour*, to dictates and pledges which tie him, in a 'serment exécrable' (line 814) or 'serment téméraire' (line 893), to Emilie and her vendetta.

Their meeting, in what is the most forceful scene of the tragedy (Act III, Scene 4), offers a fascinating contrast of personalities and moods. Emilie's calmness (compare Act IV, Scene 4) and stated unchanging nature (line 914) force Cinna to raise the issue of the 'bonté d'Auguste' (line 931), leading to her cry that she alone is beyond the Emperor's grasp. Initially Cinna responds in kind, repeating her 'Je suis toujours moi-même' (line 945), reaffirming his loyalty, and claiming sole responsibility for having kept Auguste in power. But his mood soon changes, as he wishes to become a slave to the Emperor (line 982) – a far cry from his strong attack on just such a state in Act I (line 182) and an ironical commentary on how his commitment to 'serve' his beloved has turned into 'enslavement' to her mortal enemy. Unable to move Emilie from her belief in 'un Citoyen Romain', Cinna can only argue, not *for* the Imperial system but *against* assassination and its long-term effects. Emilie's priority now seems to have shifted from vengeance to patriotism ('Je saurai bien venger mon pays et mon père', line 1018, cf. ll.156, 306), and she herself will take responsibility for carrying out the deed if Cinna is unwilling.

The latter, caught between his promise and his conscience, struggles to resolve his dilemma. With the utmost reluctance, he finally agrees to do her bidding, in a slowly delivered, dignified response which emphasises the pressure she exerts (the four 'il faut', ll.1049-51, and three 'Vous me faites...' and their antitheses, ll.1057-59), his objections (the 'Mais' of ll.1052, 1055, 1062), his description of her control as 'inhumain' (line 1055), and his decision to commit suicide after the assassination in order to redeem his damaged *gloire*. This final speech before his judgement in Act V confers considerable tragic status on Cinna. Outmanœuvred in her enthusiasm by Emilie, he here manages to focus our attention again on the central issues and arouse in us genuine tragic emotions, pity and fear.

Maxime's betrayal of the conspiracy, like Auguste's un-expected benevolence in Act II, prevents the action promised from being carried out. In the face of overwhelming evidence and Auguste's sarcastic and humiliating attacks, Cinna defends himself as best he can in Act V. His brave or foolhardy attempt to shield Emilie is quickly undone by her arrival and her claims, and he finds himself forced to explain how a promise of revenge overcame her initial lack of interest in him. Momentary disagreement gives way to unity as, on behalf of them both, Emilie expounds their common aims and demands a shared death.

Our final view of the title-character is of him falling humbly into line after Emilie's surprising conversion and gratefully accepting Auguste's additional gift of the consulate. What overall impressions does he leave? Firstly, he has no overriding political ambitions: Auguste's hypotheses about Cinna's wish to succeed him (ll.1509-16, 1534-40) and Euphorbe's similar comments (ll.753-55) prove incorrect. Indeed his actual political views are unimportant. What interests Corneille is how they clash, with those of others at different times and, in Act II, Scene 1, with the opinions which he himself previously expounded, and the psychological effects which such clashes produce. Secondly, in stressing his relationship with Pompey, he perhaps indicates, if not an inferiority complex, then a strong urge to emulate his grandfather (ll.237-38). Even in the rabble-rousing context of his address to the conspirators, this betrays the young nobleman's uncertainty about his worth and how to defend and enhance his honour.

Thirdly, his love is what forms the spring of the action. When reciprocated by Emilie at some point in the past, it resulted in her call for revenge, and during the five acts of the play it causes Cinna's mounting inner struggle and the jealousy which leads to Maxime's denunciation. And fourthly, although 'parricide' was currently used to describe anyone who committed a monstrous crime against, for example, a ruler or benefactor, the word is chosen by Cinna to indicate also his eventual feelings towards Auguste as his spiritual if not genetic father.

Self-regarding and self-dramatising, Cinna is often criticised for being two-faced, most noticeably in the consultation scene. Whatever his true political leanings, it seems a trifle ungracious to mark him down as duplicitous when he is caught completely unawares by Auguste's thoughts of abdication. He acts a part, with great conviction, at a time in the action when he cannot be said to be putting others' lives at risk. And can we talk about his readiness to see Rome enslaved when he is merely using Emilie's descriptive terms?

He has other admirable traits: courageous defiance and convincing words when cornered, leadership potential at least, and above all an underlying honesty and faithfulness which make him reaffirm his oath to Emilie despite his better judgement. Such obedience may seem demeaning or weak, but he finally restates it after having weighed up the alternatives and does so in the belief that suicide can be the only result. Were Cinna a mature adult, one could justifiably criticise several aspects of his character, as well as his at times over-precious language. But, in view of his age and inexperience, it is probably better to give him the benefit of the doubt. Like Rodrigue, like Horace too, Cinna is struggling to move successfully from youth to adulthood.

Emilie

Emilie's position is quite different from that of apparently similar characters in Corneille's previous plays. In both *Le Cid* and *Horace* the revenge-seekers – Chimène and Valère (on behalf of the murdered Camille) respectively – have a source of satisfaction in the king. At least their claims are listened to and weighed up. And each time a case is made that the guilty party, Rodrigue or Horace, has eventually done enough to extinguish the call for vengeance. In *Cinna*, the Emperor is threatened by death rather than by mere failure to enhance his power-base, and Emilie is not the complainant but the very instigator of his planned assassination. In conspiracy terms she is not just the Porcie of Scudéry's *La Mort de César* and similar tragedies on the death of Julius Caesar; she takes on the role of Porcie's husband Brute.

On the surface Emilie's part is a simple one. She calls for Auguste's head to avenge his having put her father Toranius to death twenty years earlier. The vendetta is of shorter duration, existing only since her meeting with Cinna some four years before the play starts, but it is well established. Like Hermione in *Andromaque,* seeking the murder of Pyrrhus (IV, 4, ll.1269-70), Emilie requires personal revenge (ll.101-02). But in her case the motive is the political killing of her father, while in Racine's play Hermione wants revenge for being abandoned in favour of another woman – or rather she thinks she does, but subsequently changes her mind.

Emilie's role is also different from that of Sabine, the Alban married to the Roman Horace in the play of that name. Like her, Sabine was invented for the purposes of the *intrigue,* fitting credibly into the story of the war between Rome and Alba, split emotionally between her husband and her brothers. But just as *Cinna* broadens the historico-political perspectives, moving from the city-states with their respective kings to the far-flung Roman Empire, so Sabine's largely passive role as an ironic opponent of her husband is transformed into something more passionate, more fanatical.

Emilie is young and nubile – even in the heat of her vendetta she can promise Cinna that 'mes faveurs t'attendent' (line 277) and taunt him with the comment 'Mille autres à l'envi recevraient cette loi' (line 1035). But she is not out to seduce: 'séduire' (line 1622 and elsewhere) means to deceive, to lead astray. If her passion really is greater than her hatred of the Emperor, it is not just because it provides a solution to her problem. Cinna's death would be no revenge (line 36), for 'mon cœur l'adore' (line 54) and she is his prize (line 276); her tears in Act III, Scene 5 betray her love, and in the final verbal assault on Auguste she describes herself and Cinna as 'de vrais Amants' (line 1648). This unity is not disturbed by her calling him 'tu' (in her monologue and from line 261 onwards), after an initial 'vous' to his face in Act I, Scene 3 (ll.141-44), whereas he addresses her as 'vous' throughout. As Watts points out (*4,* p.151), the familiar form was the privilege of the lady in the early French classical theatre, but not usually of the suitor, and is a further sign of her enthusiasm and drive.

At least this is the overall thrust of her passion. At times, revenge takes priority (e.g. ll.54-56) and she is prepared to contemplate Cinna's death in her service (e.g. ll.42, 133). But she does not use blackmail, merely persuasion which meets with a ready response until such time as Cinna discovers the real Auguste. Even in her strongest attack on her lover's vacillations (ll.1011-48), she can tell him that 'Je t'aime toutefois quel que tu puisses être' (line 1033), and at the end she allows Cinna to retain his share of the glory, not decrying his efforts but simply claiming her own share alongside his.

In her monologue or with Fulvie she calls her pursuit of Auguste her duty (ll.48, 57, 99, 123, 1068), but after the opening two scenes this self-imposed private task of avenging her actual father becomes a more general battle against her adoptive father and the tyranny he represents. The punishment of parricide, in its literal and wider meanings, is in her mind a self-justifying deed, crossing normal moral boundaries (ll.83, 974). There is little sign in her of any wider political views, of any feeling of public duty towards the freeing of Rome. The 'sang' which she is seeking to avenge as late as the penultimate scene is that of Toranius, not Rome.

The 'fureur' which impels Emilie along her chosen path (ll.17, 1728) explains her readiness to die (ll.140, 335, 1337, 1388, and Act V, Scene 2). But just as Cinna was a very human mixture of cool decisiveness (Act I, Scene 4) and hesitation (Act III, Scenes 3-4), so Emilie has to drop the Stoic mask at times and displays a feminine side through her fears (Act I, Scene 4) and weeping (Act III, Scene 5). She is also forced to recognise her debt to Auguste, who has given her not just financial support (line 641) but authority ('crédit', line 71). All this 'faveur' (line 69), all these 'bienfaits' (line 73), unwillingly acknowledged, compromise her ideological purity but, together with her normal human vulnerability, help in explaining her seemingly inexplicable 'conversion' in the final scene.

The play could have ended with Auguste's pardon, but it is important that the conspirators recognise and react to the clemency. Emilie is their first and main spokesman, leaving Cinna and Maxime to say little and Livie to convey the historical fact of the Emperor's apotheosis. What makes Emilie speak as she does, laying down her arms and accepting the Emperor's forgiveness? There is a predictably wide range of interpretations. Some, like S. Doubrovsky (*16*, p.216), believe that she suddenly sees and accepts the need for monarchy. Others (L. Herland, *26*, p.143; A. Georges, *20*, p.127) believe she experiences the intervention of divine grace. For R. Zuber, she has finally overcome her 'traumatisme d'enfance' (*49*, p.275). M. Descotes (*15*, p.182) talks of her 'agenouillement' or bowing before the authority of Auguste in a *coup de théâtre* which the critic finds impossible to explain, while more recently the same view has been re-expressed by Leiner and Bayne as Emilie subordinating herself to a man, now recognised as her superior, part of the misogyny of the French pre-classical era (*29*, pp.205-07). Yet other commentators talk of confusion between her personal ethos (the dictates of her vengeance) and her opinion about the best form of government for Rome. For O. de Mourgues there is a basic absurdity in her personal values, so much so that they are 'bound to be altogether reversed at one blow' after Auguste's clemency (*35*, p.55).

However, if we believe that her real motive at all times is vengeance and not Rome's greater good, any self-contradiction in her attitudes is much less apparent. The attacks which Emilie makes on 'la tyrannie' are not general but specific, aimed at Auguste as her father's murderer, not as Rome's current emperor. Her motives remain personal, and the vision she regains at the end of the play opens her eyes to his individual qualities of magnanimity. The problem of Emilie and her change of mind seems less daunting than that of the clemency itself, examined in the next chapter. A dispassionate study of Corneille's text suggests that, within this 'adorable Furie', as Guez de Balzac will call her, lies a young woman who, despite her monomania, is, as he says, essentially reasonable. Although offered at the end no more than the husband granted to her in Act II, she has shown enough devotion to Cinna to heed Auguste's statement 'Te rendant un époux, je te rends plus qu'un père' (line 1714) and to accept his challenge to overcome her anger. Like Chimène she has done enough to prove her point and is convinced, on the evidence of Auguste's change of heart, that further resistance would damage her own and Cinna's future. Especially

given her human qualities and failings, it does not seem incoherent to
try to reconcile her final response with her earlier vengeance-
seeking. Of course she goes beyond mere acceptance of the
clemency, repents of her crime, and undertakes to serve Auguste
with an 'ardeur' which matches her love and her previous 'fureur'.
Does that not fit in with her nature which, as we have noted, is to do
nothing by halves?

The French Revolution heightened interest in the political
debate contained within *Cinna* at the expense of the love plot, and
this led both actors and audiences to focus on Auguste rather than on
Cinna and Emilie, an emphasis which is still apparent in modern
productions. During the seventeenth and eighteenth centuries,
however, what had gripped imaginations had been the relationship
between the two chief conspirators and its happy outcome. The
Prince de Conti commented in his *Traité de la comédie* of 1666 that
one's admiration must go to 'toutes les choses tendres et passionnées
que [Cinna] dit à Emilie' and she to him, rather than to Auguste's
clemency, 'à laquelle on pense peu, et dont aucun des spectateurs n'a
jamais songé à faire l'éloge en sortant de la Comédie' (*34*, p.96).
That this view was not untypical of Corneille's day is confirmed by
Guez de Balzac's warm letter to the author days after receiving an
advance copy of *Cinna*. The discerning critic writes enthusiastically
about the play and about Corneille's success in conveying an
appropriate feeling of Romanness which even improves on the
original: 'Aux endroits où Rome est de brique, vous la rebâtissez de
marbre'. He has particular praise for Sabine (*Horace*) and for Emilie,
both invented characters, 'les principaux ornements de vos deux
Poèmes', 'ces Romaines de votre façon'. He finds Emilie especially
well drawn, more so than Cinna, who himself is better in Corneille
than in Seneca. There is no reaction at all to Auguste, except
indirectly when Balzac lauds Emilie's desire to 'sacrifier à son Père
une victime qui serait trop grande pour Jupiter même' (*1*, I, pp.1056-
57). Times, preferences and interpretations change, and most
present-day audiences and readers feel less attracted by the heroics of
the conspirators than by the inner confusion of their principal victim.

4. Victims

Into this category I shall put the obvious Auguste, but also Livie, who would lose much by his death, and, more controversially, Maxime's freedman, adviser and confidant, Euphorbe.

Euphorbe

The function of three of the four minor characters in *Cinna* is easily assessed. Two of the three *affranchis*, Polyclète and Evandre, have no more than walk-on parts. Fulvie states a morally acceptable opinion to her mistress in Act I, Scene 2, the better to throw into sharp relief Emilie's amoral or egoistic response. Subsequently the confidante fulfils minor, conventional roles as comforter (Act III, Scene 5) and bearer of both precise and vague news, thus contributing to the suspense element in the plot (Act IV, Scene 4). Maxime's former slave, on the other hand, although speaking just sixty-two lines, has a more substantial part to play.

Unlike Fulvie, who accompanies Emilie in all but one of her ten scenes, Euphorbe does not shadow his master. His two interventions, in Act III, Scene 1 and again during the third interval and in Act IV, Scene 1 with Auguste, demonstrate widely differing qualities of mind and personality: his astuteness, his devotion, but also the ease with which he first guides, then tempts and finally perverts Maxime. While the latter remains stunned by the reasons which Cinna has just given him for the conspiracy, Euphorbe recognises, as Fulvie had, the inherent goodness of the Emperor: as he says to Maxime, deprived of their present leader 'tous vos Conjurés deviendraient ses amis' (line 716). Without the motive provided by his love of Emilie, Cinna, too, 'aimerait César' (line 747). Although taken completely by surprise by Maxime's revelation .of his rivalry in love, Euphorbe does not need to probe the details (reserved for Maxime's encounter with Emilie, Act IV, Scene 5) in order to grasp the implications. Then again, although excluded from the deliberation scene, he has noticed and understood, much more clearly than his master could, the Emperor's disillusionment, the reason why he now inspires respect, even love: 'Auguste s'est lassé d'être si rigoureux' (line 764).

Maxime's instinctive reaction is to blame the hypocrisy of Cinna, 'qui n'agit que pour soi, feignant d'agir pour Rome' (line 718). In so doing, he makes clear his own deep-seated egoism, his belief that he is entitled to Emilie, and his unwillingness to, as he puts it, self-destruct (line 727). At least initially, Euphorbe could be said to do no more than act logically in recommending that Maxime look after his own interests, as Cinna had done, and denounce the leader of the conspiracy. Revealing all to Auguste is simply the more realistic option, one which has the double advantage of saving the life of a benevolent Emperor and of increasing his gratitude and hence (perhaps) his willingness to grant Emilie to Maxime.

Thus far, the confidant perhaps does little more than guide his master, reusing his words ('agir', 'dessein', 'perdre', 'rival', 'amitié') to put a different perspective on the situation. But where many critics see Euphorbe turn into a *mauvais conseiller* is when he reacts to Maxime's hesitation at betraying not just a co-conspirator but a friend. The freedman's responses, couched in *sentences* as if they were general truths (ll.735, 736, 742), now emphasise passion over politics, the lovable 'Maîtresse' before the Imperial 'Maître' (line 738). Euphorbe is intelligent enough to see that at this stage Maxime is more concerned with his personal loss than with any ideological differences he may have with Cinna. He repeats Maxime's allegations about Cinna's self-interest (ll.745-46) and – correctly, as it later transpires – points out Cinna's intrinsic affection for Auguste and his lack of disinterestedness, the cause of what he terms the conspirator's 'lâcheté' (line 744). Only after allowing these recycled ideas to sink in does Euphorbe broach a new matter, Cinna's possible political ambitions, which could involve the subjection of Rome and even Maxime's death (ll.749-56).

While Cinna's secretiveness about the true motive for the conspiracy is given as the cause of Euphorbe's suggestion (ll.750-52), nothing in the play indicates that Cinna wishes to advance his own political cause. Euphorbe may simply be less well-informed than we or Maxime are and is here airing his genuine opinion or hazarding a guess. On the other hand, his insinuations could be seen as a Machiavellian attempt to save his own skin and even promote some personal cause by influencing his very vulnerable master. What is noticeable at this stage is Maxime's immediate acceptance of the innuendo. There are none of the earlier moral scruples about betrayal, no discussion precedes his question which is about means rather than ends: 'Mais comment l'accuser [Cinna] sans nommer tout le reste?' (line 757). He has some no doubt genuine concerns for the risks which the minor co-conspirators would run following denunciation of their leader. Euphorbe has a ready answer to this (ll.764-68) but Maxime rejects it, not for its own sake but because he anticipates that clemency from Auguste would not guarantee him Emilie, whose heart and not just hand he must win.

When Act III opens, Maxime can scarcely be said to be panic-stricken, having had some time since Cinna's explanation to come to terms with the new realities. His readiness to consider Euphorbe's plan seriously shows that the freedman is merely expressing thoughts which have already crossed his mind. Even when Euphorbe bluntly confesses that the ploy is basically a means of gaining time, his master does not abandon the project. His concern might appear to be for Emilie (ll.785-86), but the following couplet demonstrates that it is only for himself and his thwarted love.

Two wrongs do not make a right, and Euphorbe is no angel, but equally a close study of his role in this scene could lead us to conclude that he does no more than propose the obvious, what he considers to be in the best interests of his master as the latter has outlined them. Passion dominates Maxime's early remarks, almost fusing with the assassination plot when Cinna's prior love is seen as Maxime's 'perte' and taking precedence over the conspiracy in the order of events (ll.721-28). Euphorbe could thus be said to follow – or be led – rather than to lead in the attempted resolution of

Maxime's dilemma. In particular he has a clear understanding of Cinna's real motives, going beyond Maxime's analysis of his friend, and this perspicacity, together with a freedman's desire to say what his master wants to hear, encourages him to exceed the known facts and indulge in some wild speculation.

The denunciation of the conspiracy, or rather of Cinna's and Maxime's role in it, is undertaken by Euphorbe. This is in line with seventeenth-century thinking that responsibility for such dastardly action should be transferred from a major to a minor figure, thus preserving the proprieties. But it is Maxime who, at the end of Act III, Scene 1, arranges to see Euphorbe 'dans peu' and who must therefore be assumed to have given the plan his final approval. The *affranchi* enunciates what Maxime dislikes yet thinks, but then awaits orders before proceeding.

In Act IV, although he has denounced both Cinna and Maxime, the latter is partly exonerated, as his freedman had anticipated, for the betrayal of the conspiracy is seen by the Emperor as proof of Maxime's repentance (line 1088). This provides a cue for Euphorbe to invent similar remorse among the co-conspirators and to emphasise the continuing active plotting of Cinna. What he has not done in his report is to mention Emilie's involvement, far less her leading role. This deliberate omission can be judged in two ways: as protection of the person Maxime claims to love, or as a signal that Euphorbe realises only too well that Emilie would not seek to hide her crime but would, as a martyr, be tempted to bring all involved crashing down along with her. In either case, his silence contributes to the immediate well-being of his master. Why then does he spin the elaborate yarn of Maxime's suicide by drowning (ll.1103-14), an account which Corneille actually strengthened in his 1660 revisions?

It cannot be simply in order that Auguste is moved to pronounce a line which can be seen as a forerunner of his clemency: 'Il n'est crime envers moi qu'un repentir n'efface' (line 1117). Later in Act IV Maxime will explain to Emilie that 'Se voyant arrêté, la trame découverte, / [Euphorbe] a feint ce trépas pour empêcher ma perte' (ll.1317-18). There is no truth in this feeble excuse. Cinna has been summoned by Auguste (via the instruction to Polyclète, line

1099, confirmed by Fulvie, ll.1277-80), but the decision to reveal the conspiracy was Maxime's, implemented by Euphorbe. It can only be that the freedman is trying to give his master time to reorganise his personal life. Maxime is unlikely to have had the wit to contribute to such a scenario, one which the dramatist may have playfully decided to render even more melodramatic as a sign that he recognised the attraction to audiences of an improbable 'death' leading to an early 'resurrection'. If nothing else, the account underlines the gullibility and thus the weakness of Auguste at this point, still rocked by the news of his advisers' treachery.

If excessive devotion to Maxime and his cause is thus apparent in some of Euphorbe's actions, the sentence which his master seeks to have passed on him is unduly harsh, however much seventeenth-century audiences may have been swayed by comments about a former slave being unable to change his spots (ll.1408-12). The request for torture had, of course, been thoroughly prepared by Maxime's soliloquy where, apostrophising Euphorbe, he promised to allow 'mes ressentiments / De te sacrifier aux yeux des deux Amants' (ll.1419-20), to 'laver le forfait de t'avoir écouté' (line 1424). Both in Act IV and again in the final scene the conspirator's determination to commit suicide thereafter as atonement for his sin of treason is devalued by his description of Euphorbe as 'ce traître', worthy of punishment (ll.1690-92, cf. line 1416).

The role played by Euphorbe is thus a trifle more subtle than is often admitted. While he must bear responsibility for some of the action, the more important elements can rightly be attributed to Maxime, his social if not moral superior. Before we accept the emancipated slave as degenerate, it is necessary to compare him with, say, the Narcisse of Racine's *Britannicus* (1669). There is in fact no comparison.

Livie

Livie's role, although small, is crucial to our understanding of the play. Yet in eighteenth- and early nineteenth-century France the part was excised as being redundant, and Voltaire, a not insensitive commentator on several of Corneille's plays, could write that her arrival was both late and unnecessary, that her advice detracted from Auguste's ability to take the clemency decision himself, and that his eventual granting of pardon, after a 'comic' rejection of his wife's advice, was nothing if not demeaning (9, vol.54, pp.155-56).

There is more to the Empress's influence than what she says in her three scenes (Act IV, Scene 3; Act V, Scenes 2 and 3). She may speak only seventy-four lines in all, but her off-stage presence and activities are unusually important. It is clear that Auguste keeps his wife informed of major political developments, such as his reluctant decision not to abdicate (ll.646, 909). We have seen earlier how the two women have a relationship, too. Significantly, the first mention of Livie in the play is Emilie's wish to, as it were, supplant her, but only in order to gain immediate access to the man she might herself have to kill (ll.81-82). Subsequently Emilie hopes to use her friendship to exert influence through Livie at a time of apparent crisis (ll.346-48), and she is accompanied by her when she appears in front of Auguste in Act V, Scene 2. During Act II and much of Act III she has been in the Empress's apartments – logically enough in one sense, since Auguste treats her as his adoptive daughter, but not without obvious irony, too.

While her husband is racked with doubts in Act IV, Livie is being told by Euphorbe what Maxime had wanted Auguste to hear (ll.1195-96). These references in the text to offstage meetings which Livie has with Auguste, with Emilie and with Euphorbe are carefully documented. Not so is any encounter between Livie and Auguste during the last interval such as the Empress appears to seek at the end of Act IV, Scene 3. Although certain critics, among them P. J. Yarrow (48, pp.549-50), assume it must take place by virtue of having been desired, there is no mention of it at all in Act V. The clemency appears not to be influenced at that late stage by further direct persuasion by Livie.

The first *Discours* tells us that Livie is a person 'qui console et conseille son mari' (1, III, p.136). This is true, but not the whole truth. Her main role in the play itself is to propose a form of clemency which is immediately rejected by her husband, for reasons which we can only extrapolate from his other remarks. Livie has three fairly distinct aims in mind when speaking with Auguste in Act IV, just minutes after hearing of the foiled conspiracy. She suggests that clemency would consolidate the Emperor's political power, that it would add to his renown, and that the self-mastery needed to offer it would augment his personal moral worth. In angrily dismissing her proposal and her subsequent entreaty that he not contemplate abdication, Auguste accuses her of having political ambitions (ll.1256, 1261). But there is no evidence whatsoever to suggest that this is what motivates Livie. She is acting, not for self-aggrandisement or indeed in defence of Cinna, whose actions she must deplore, but on behalf of Auguste, strengthening his resolve by referring to the past crimes of which he is all too conscious and dismissing them as those of a previous persona – Octavian, not Augustus. In Act V, Scene 2 she argues (ll.1605-16) that his past deeds were, in any case, absolved by the mere assumption of imperial power, which brings with it retrospective immunity: the end, which is good (stable, absolute government), justifies even the most dubious of means. Yet as and when stated, these Machiavellian principles, in line with much seventeenth-century thinking, have little effect on her husband – the discussion switches to a *concours de générosité* between Emilie and Cinna and the scene ends with Auguste's second threats of punishment.

In advocating a softer line, Livie gave no thought to repentance by Cinna, a further sign that her main preoccupation is consolidation of Auguste's power and preservation of the Empire rather than personal moral cleansing. Contrition, however, is what the Emperor wanted: he had said as much with reference to Maxime in Act IV, Scene 1 (line 1117), and Emilie's eventual recognition of guilt and feelings of remorse (ll.1717, 1719), no doubt shared by the less articulate Cinna and Maxime, help to underscore the rightness of the pardon. For it brings out the contrast between Auguste's magnanimous effacement of the conspirators' crime and the dubious desire of Livie to wipe from the historical record all the crimes of Octave.

There remains Livie's last intervention in the play (ll.1753-74), lines which many find difficult to interpret or accept. The 'céleste flamme' which she claims illuminates her soul appears merely to confirm as future certainties the items which in Act IV she had identified as desirable attributes which clemency would bring. Auguste will live without fear of further assassination attempts, the Romans are wedded to imperial government, and his apotheosis is being prepared. Her words are no doubt dramatically useful, for they offer a perspective into the future, beyond the clemency and the conspirators' acceptance of it. But they also show that her sole concern, even at this late stage, is with political matters. The fulsome tone, in particular of lines 1770-72, owes much to Antoine's comments following a funeral oration in praise of Julius Caesar in Act V, Scene 6 of Scudéry's *La Mort de César* or to Tristan L'Hermite's tragedy *La Marianne,* performed at the Marais in 1636, where the closing moments (Act V, Scene 3) show the distraught king Hérode 'seeing' the apotheosis of his wife Marianne whom he has just had put to death, this pagan vision then being followed by a kind of Christian assumption of the executed queen into Heaven.

One could argue that Corneille includes the spectacular and historical but hackneyed device of the deification, not of a dead but of a living person, as a tongue-in-cheek attempt to outdo his contemporary rival dramatists. For is it not with a light touch of irony that Auguste replies to Livie's utterances in a curt couplet: 'J'en accepte l'augure et j'ose l'espérer, / Ainsi toujours les Dieux vous daignent inspirer' (ll.1775-76)? If, as argued elsewhere in this analysis, divine intervention is nowhere evident in the play, the Emperor at least knows how to humour his wife and her prophetic foibles before turning to more important business such as the marriage the next day (line 1740) of Cinna and Emilie. But Livie's final speech does serve to confirm the legitimacy of Auguste. Despite his having usurped power and committed atrocities while acting as a tyrant, his subsequent conduct has made him an acceptable, even respected monarch. As the curtain falls, it is important that we should be left not just with the reassurance of an almost miraculous clemency and series of 'conversions' but with a statement that the Empire is in legitimised hands.

Auguste

If Euphorbe and in particular Livie can lay only minor claim to victim status, Auguste is a more substantial and difficult figure to come to terms with. For he is presented under a range of guises, three of them mentioned by Cinna in line 159: 'Au seul nom de César, d'Auguste, et d'Empereur'. To these must be added Octave, occurring nine times in the text and used by all the main characters and Euphorbe.

The future Augustus was born in 63 BC as Gaius Octavius; like all subsequent Roman emperors, he was called Caesar following the assassination of Julius Caesar in 44 BC, when he changed Octavius to Octavianus. He gained the title of Imperator or military leader some six years later, using it as a first name (Imperator Caesar). The name Augustus was acquired in 27 BC.

In *Cinna*, 'César' designates Julius Caesar (ll.427, 430 and elsewhere), as does 'le grand César' (ll.378, 597), but just as often it is used of the adoptive son. The name in Corneille is neutral, not referring to any particular period in the life and career of Augustus; the two syllables simply provide a convenient alternative to the three of 'l'Empereur' and the three (sometimes two) of 'Auguste'. 'Octave', on the other hand, carries two meanings. Like 'César' it can be an all-purpose title, used of the present-day Auguste (as in ll.753, 909, 1390), but it also relates specifically to the Octavius/Octavianus period in Augustus's earlier life: the Emperor chooses it in his soliloquy (ll.1130, 1169), and Livie makes the same distinction even more explicit when she says that the death of Toranius 'fut un crime d'Octave, et non de l'Empereur' (line 1608).

This confusion or at least sequence of different titles and functions may seem at odds with the uniqueness claimed for the role by Corneille in 1660 in an interesting passage of the *Examen* to his early play *Clitandre* (*1*, I, pp.102-03) where he is describing the effectiveness of the King and his son in that tragi-comedy. The playwright distinguishes three ways in which a ruler can appear on the stage: 'comme Roi, comme homme, et comme Juge, quelquefois avec deux de ces qualités, quelquefois toutes les trois ensemble'. The ruler-judge is like Alcandre in *Clitandre* or Don Fernand in *Le Cid* (or, one might add, Tulle in *Horace*), 'introduit sans aucun intérêt pour son Etat, ni pour sa personne, ni pour ses affections, mais seulement pour régler celui des autres'. Contrasting with this arbitration function is that of the human ruler, who 'n'a que l'intérêt d'une passion à suivre ou à vaincre, sans aucun péril pour son Etat'. The Emperor in *Cinna* is given as an example of the ruler as monarch, 'quand il n'a intérêt qu'à la conservation de son Trône, ou de sa vie, qu'on attaque pour changer l'Etat, sans avoir l'esprit agité d'aucune passion particulière'. Although this outline of single functions is somewhat schematic, it is true that Auguste's overriding concern is not with personal matters but with the State and his position in it; the judicial role which he plays in Act V is a direct and necessary consequence of that concern.

More important, however, than any mere title or change in name is the question of identity. It is here that, in Corneille's hands, Auguste becomes both a figure of great complexity and one who finally achieves considerable coherence. His twenty years of power (line 1248) have seen him forced into a series of personas, mentioned by his attackers, by his wife, and in his Act IV soliloquy. Even earlier, Act V tells us, there had been enmity between his adoptive father, Julius Caesar, and Cinna's father Lucius Cornelius Cinna, who was the brother-in-law of Caesar and son-in-law of Pompey the Great. Cinna the son thus had a congenital hatred of Augustus carried in his blood, as the Emperor reminds him : 'Tu fus mon ennemi, même avant que de naître / [...] / Ce sang qui t'avait fait du contraire parti' (ll.1441, 1444).

Octave and Auguste, then: two consecutive stages of the career and personality of Corneille's character. By everyone's account, including his own, Octave was a bloodthirsty monster, who personally undertook (or at least oversaw) the killing of Emilie's father as a first step on the climb to imperial power (ll.11-12). For Emilie he is simply 'un ennemi' (line 40), and, like Chimène insistently demanding the head of Rodrigue who had just killed her father in a duel of honour (*Le Cid*), she seeks a straightforward solution: his death at the hands of Cinna, an eye for an eye, for revenge knows no moral laws and his daily benefactions to his adoptive daughter are just so many unacceptable bribes from a tyrant (line 108).

It soon transpires that the consultation in Act II concerns two technically discrete matters, Auguste's personal abdication, and a possible change of political system for Rome. Most of Auguste's opening speech is devoted to the first issue: the earlier examples of Sulla and Julius Caesar are offered as conflicting and in any case inexact models, and a reminder is given (ll.394-95) of his previous but indecisive consultation with Agrippa and Maecenas, the first advising him to abdicate, the latter recommending that he stay in power. Line 404 summarises the personal question he is now putting to Cinna and Maxime, but lines 401-02 clearly foresee that a recommendation that he step down would or might result in a switch to Republican government.

Having listened to his advisers, Auguste decides with great misgivings to retain power, not out of personal ambition but in service to a cause which is beyond himself: 'Mon repos m'est bien cher, mais Rome est la plus forte / [...] / Je consens à me perdre afin de la sauver' (ll.622, 624). The debate has not just concerned the best type of government or given us insight into how, in turn, Cinna and Maxime cope with their unexpected situation. The fact that it has taken place at all, and that the Emperor is visibly loath to carry on, confer on him a new level of legitimacy. For, as a tyrant-usurper, his status has been uncertain. Fair government by a usurper would be seen by independent observers in seventeenth-century France as making that person a just ruler, his authority becoming legitimate because it has proved to be stable and established. The moral change which thus occurs in Act II, Scene 1 when Auguste puts his authority on the line explains part of the apparent shift in interest which occurs from then on. Cinna's ambition, despite his doubts, and Maxime's conspiring are on a different plane from that now inhabited by the

Emperor, his past criminality gradually losing its force as he offers himself to radical change.

This renewal is not, of course, recognised by the conspirators. Cinna talks enthusiastically about the change (ll.414, 419-26), yet the irony behind the hypocrisy of his words is clear to impartial observers like the audience. Maxime, too, briefly mentions Auguste's 'juste conquête' (ll.443-46), but he was forced into the admission by Cinna and he soon moves on to state his Republican ideals. It is noticeable at this stage how little Auguste gives away about his real past, making only passing reference to his earlier savagery in euphemisms such as 'tant de peine et de sang' (line 360) or the 'sévérité' with which he treated Emilie's father (line 640), a result of 'la nécessité' or reason of State, not of his desire. As a result there is no hint in Act II of any remorse, a term used by Cinna (line 414) and taken up by Maxime (line 465). The Emperor's initial reticence heightens the effect of the self-examination he conducts following discovery of the conspiracy. There the flood-gates will open and he will be entirely frank with himself. The coincidence in time of his discovery of the plot and his own admission of criminality in turn lends greater realism to the subsequent clemency: had he been forced to admit his past to himself and the public earlier, the treachery of his advisers and adoptive daughter might not have been so easy to forgive.

The tyranny of Auguste is what Cinna refers to, at least when he is with Emilie in Act I or later with Maxime, where he has to keep up his pretence (ll.663, 690, 700). There he rails against the thought of the Emperor getting away with mere remorse (line 656), with 'un lâche repentir' (line 658). What strikes us about Auguste in Act IV is the readiness with which he would accept contrition from the guilty Maxime, yet the absence of remorse in his own self-examination (Act IV, Scene 2). That wide-ranging, tormented soliloquy repeats (line 1124) the first thought Auguste had had on learning of the treachery, the loss of friends (line 1081), and is pitiless in bringing out his own bloody past, the grounds for the conspiracy, and the pointlessness of further wholesale bloodshed. But significantly there are no expressions of regret, and the lengthy debate about suicide as the only solution gives way to thoughts of vengeance and of a spectacular death for Cinna.

The monologue may end in complete indecision, but some things become clear as the Emperor moves towards confronting first his wife, then the guilty parties. There can be no doubt about the effect his past has had, and continues to have, on him; his inability to erase the harrowing memories is clear from the two-thirds and more of the speech devoted to them. Secondly, he concludes in his despair that the conspirators, excluding Cinna, are largely justified and that general punishment would serve no purpose. But thirdly, the putting to death of Cinna, believed to be the unrepentant ringleader, is talked about only in conjunction with Auguste's own death through suicide (ll.1180-85), an exit 'avec éclat' (line 1179) which would remove the temptation of further widespread slaughter ('tout perdre', line 1176) and satisfy Rome's hatred of him (line 1186), while in a way circumventing it.

It is the very recent and sudden loss of trust in a former friend, and his own previously stated lack of further political ambition, which are the key factors in Auguste's rejection of Livie's clemency proposal (Act IV, Scene 3). Her advice that he avoid bloodshed coincides with his general thinking but not with his decision to single out Cinna, while his 'Renommée' (line 1214) has been of no concern to him since before Act II. His words to his wife are blunt, perhaps understandably so given his emotional turmoil in the two previous scenes and her excessively pragmatic turn of mind. For the Emperor, his duty is clear: the mere thought of regicide is a 'crime d'Etat' and requires punishment, what he interestingly terms revenge (ll.1251-54).

By the start of the interrogations in Act V, time (three scenes plus an interval), if not further discussion with Livie (what more could she add?), has allowed him to regain the composure he demonstrated in Act II. But he has not yet reached any decision. Despite some critics' attempts to interpret his self-assuredness as proof that clemency is a foregone conclusion and that he is playing cat-and-mouse with Cinna for pure (or perverse) enjoyment before announcing the good news, Corneille's text simply contradicts this reading (see *22, 23*). The Emperor may be hoping that Cinna will seek the same self-knowledge that he himself sought (line 1517, cf. line 1130) and even reach repentance (line 1558), but these passing references to a source of possible forgiveness are overwhelmed by more direct language. Reminders by Auguste of his benefactions (ll.1435-76), detailed exposure of the assassination plans (ll.1482-96), and some hard-hitting questions and ironical remarks about motives (ll.1499-1516) precede a humiliating assurance that Cinna would be as nothing without his support. The conspirator's fearless response ('Seigneur, je suis Romain, et du sang de Pompée', line 1546) and complete lack of remorse leave Auguste no room to manœuvre; his conclusion is crystal-clear: 'Tu sais ce qui t'es dû, tu vois que je sais tout, / Fais ton Arrêt toi-même, et choisis tes supplices' (ll.1560-61).

The discovery that Emilie is caught up in the treachery, not just on its fringes but as 'la cause, et le salaire' (line 1566), elicits a modified version of Julius Caesar's alleged cry (line 1564). The contest between Emilie and Cinna in claiming sole responsibility for the conspiracy gives Auguste time to reflect, but again his response leaves little room for doubt. Emilie's taunt that she be united with Cinna, that is, in death, is taken up twice by the Emperor who recognises the love which has existed between the pair for several years (line 1660) but promises that the world will be paralysed with fear by a punishment which matches the crime:

> Et que tout l'Univers, sachant ce qui m'anime,
> S'étonne du supplice aussi bien que du crime.
>   (ll.1661-62)

The seventeenth-century use of *s'étonner* here (like *étonner* in ll.123, 661 and possibly 955) makes it virtually certain that Auguste is not planning a pleasant surprise such as forgiveness and marriage. Rather, as the language of lines 1657-58 suggests, he has lost all patience with their insubordination and is preparing their fearful torture and death.

The third and final stage of Auguste's suffering seems something of an anti-climax, the reappearance, as in tragi-comedy or the pastoral novel, of a man believed drowned, come to express his abject contrition. Yet Maxime, the Emperor's last resort (line 1663) and sole remaining friend (line 1665), sees himself as the most guilty of all, with jealousy of Cinna and betrayal of him and his beloved Emilie adding to the earlier crime of *lèse-majesté*. Far from seeking a martyr's death, as Cinna and Emilie had done, he vows to have Euphorbe punished and then take his own life (line 1692).

And so to the clemency. Faced with almost as many analyses of it as there have been critics, what can the modern reader or theatre-goer do? My suggestion would be to look at the range of explanations, reject any which are clearly wrong (because founded on factually incorrect or heavily biased evidence), and then consider at some length the remaining possibles. As in all literary study, it is likely that this important piece of the jigsaw will fall into place eventually, that consistency of interpretation will be achieved, in other words that Auguste's motives here can, in retrospect, be seen to be compatible with his earlier actions.

For some, Auguste's is a calculated political gesture, even a trick. Napoleon, not the greatest dramatic critic, claimed that in a performance which he attended, the actor Monvel who played the Emperor 'prononça le: "Soyons amis, Cinna" d'un ton si habile et si rusé que je compris que cette action n'était que la feinte d'un tyran' (*1*, I, pp.1588-89). At perhaps the other extreme, several commentators, among them A. Stegmann (*44*, vol.II, p.585 – but cf. p.587), J. Maurens (*31*, pp.273-76), and R.J. Nelson (*37*, p.321), believe that Auguste acts as a consequence of divine providence or inspiration, even as a result of divine grace (D. Clarke, *12*, p.336; G. Couton, *14*, p.67; R. Jasinski, *27*, p.127). P.J. Yarrow (*48*, p.550) interprets it as a mixture of ordinary psychology and inspiration from above. Somewhere in between the influences of trickery and the supernatural come those who see the clemency as a product of pride (S. Doubrovsky, *16*, p.214), or as a bid by Auguste to establish himself as 'le maître des cœurs' (M. Prigent, *42*, p.67), or to be a source of recognition and of imitation (H. Phillips, *39*, p.168). Others believe it to be not the triumph of will-power but the victory of prudence (F.E. Sutcliffe, *45*, p.249).

The theme of clemency is not new in Corneille. His two previous plays had shown characters found guilty of wrong-doing but pardoned for political reasons. In *Le Cid*, Chimène is all but persuaded by King Fernand that Rodrigue, killer of her father in a duel of honour, has by his subsequent services to the State redeemed himself and earned her respect and love. The title-character of *Horace*, who emerges victorious from a representative combat opposing Rome and Alba and then sullies his reputation by murdering his sister, betrothed to one of the enemy, is exonerated by the Roman King Tulle, concerned, like Fernand, to reward a person who acts to defend his country but conscious, too, of his own weakness as ruler.

This is where *Cinna* offers a quite different perspective. Auguste is not a fringe character like the earlier kings, but at the heart of the plot, as both the long-term cause and the immediate target of the conspiracy threat. Nor is he normally weak, and he is certainly not faced now with feats of courage which invert the subject/monarch relationship. He has had a mixed track record, repressive early on but more conciliatory of late, exercising power in morally acceptable ways which guaranteed stability, and can therefore think that he has met the prerequisites of a certain kind of legitimacy. The conspiracy is for him as much a huge disappointment as it is a monstrous crime. The faithlessness of his two friends and close advisers and of his adoptive daughter hits hard:

> En est-ce assez, ô Ciel, et le Sort pour me nuire
> A-t-il quelqu'un des miens qu'il veuille encor séduire?
> Qu'il joigne à ses efforts le secours des Enfers,
> Je suis maître de moi comme de l'Univers.
> Je le suis, je veux l'être. O Siècles, ô Mémoire,
> Conservez à jamais ma dernière victoire,
> Je triomphe aujourd'hui du plus juste courroux
> De qui le souvenir puisse aller jusqu'à vous.

Soyons amis, Cinna...

(ll.1693-1701)

How is this 'supreme (not last or latest) victory' over 'legitimate anger' achieved? In the text it occurs between lines 1695 and 1696, in the self-mastery which equals and, in a sense, replaces his mastery of the world already mentioned by Cinna (line 440) and Maxime (line 496). It would seem to be no tactical manœuvre, as Napoleon thought, even if, in retrospect, we can see that the clemency effectively neutralises the present and future conspirators. Nor, as the next chapter will perhaps show, is there divine intervention. Rather than being a conscious attempt at self-surpassing or a sign of inherent weakness, Auguste's action appears to be instinctive, occurring literally from one moment, one line to the next, the sort of unthinking but inspired gesture which is familiar from real life and which, with the benefit of hindsight, is seen to offer the ideal solution. Paradoxically he comes to this improbable decision when, and only when, his last main political and emotional support, the trust and friendship of Maxime, has been kicked away. And significantly it is friendship which is his first thought as he emerges from the episode: 'Soyons amis, Cinna, c'est moi qui t'en convie' (line 1701).

This extraordinary response to an assassination plot underlines the loneliness of the holders of influence and their dependence on self above all. In Act II Auguste had identified the problem of relinquishing power: 'Et monté sur le faîte il [notre esprit] aspire à descendre' (line 370). Less often quoted are the preceding lines:

Et comme notre esprit jusqu'au dernier soupir
Toujours vers quelque objet pousse quelque désir,
Il se ramène en soi n'ayant plus où se prendre.
(ll.367-69)

Seeking self-knowledge and self-sufficiency (cf. line 1130), the human mind runs out of options and feeds on itself. Relationships are one of the few avenues left. After his clemency Auguste appears to

heap further political rewards on Cinna (ll.1709-10), restoring
Maxime to his former position of counsellor (line 1737) and bidding
Emilie accept Cinna's new 'illustre rang' (line 1711). But his real
aim is other and twofold: to regain his friends (line 1736) and to
consign the events of the preceding hours to oblivion (line 1780), 'un
oubli magnanime' (line 1733) which is a far cry from what he was
planning only a few scenes earlier (line 1157).

5. Tragedy

It is not only the absence of dead bodies which gives *Cinna* its particular flavour. The death of one or more characters was not a requirement of seventeenth-century French tragedy: indeed, one of the most obviously tragic plays of the period, Racine's *Bérénice* (1670), ends with the agreed separation of three characters, the Jewish queen, the Roman emperor who loves but is prevented from marrying her, and the king of Comagene who has an unreciprocated passion for her too. That tragedy, Racine's *Cinna* in the sense that it has a straightforward structure and strong internal logic, creates in its audience what its writer calls 'cette tristesse majestueuse qui fait tout le plaisir de la tragédie', an aura of profound melancholy resulting from the human decisions forced on the unhappy trio.

In very few Corneille plays, and certainly none from the 1630s or 1640s, could a feeling of majestic sadness be said to prevail. His characters are active, able and willing to shape their own destinies rather than rely on, or succumb to, the power of fate. In *Cinna*, both conspirators and victims make plans, control their lives, and assume that they must live by their decisions.

This atmosphere is aided by Corneille's thoughts on suitable subjects for tragedy. He tells us in the first of the three *Discours* of 1660 that 'les grands sujets qui remuent fortement les passions [...] doivent toujours aller au-delà du vraisemblable' (*1*, III, p.118). Back in 1647, in the *Au lecteur* to *Héraclius*, he had written in similar vein: 'l'action étant vraie [...], il ne faut plus s'informer si elle est vraisemblable, étant certain que toutes les vérités sont recevables dans la poésie [...]. J'irai plus outre, et quoique peut-être on voudra prendre cette proposition pour un paradoxe, je ne craindrai point d'avancer que le sujet d'une belle tragédie doit n'être pas vraisemblable' (*1*, II, p.357). This insistence that the basic subject-matter of a play which arouses the tragic emotions should go beyond mere plausibility and come from history or legend, however incredible, sets Corneille against commentators such as the abbé d'Aubignac who, in *La Pratique du théâtre* (1657), had argued that history, historical truth by itself, was unsuitable for the stage because 'il y a bien des choses véritables qui n'y doivent pas être vues, et beaucoup qui n'y peuvent pas être représentées [...]. Ce n'est pas que les choses véritables et possibles soient bannies du théâtre, mais elles n'y sont reçues qu'en tant qu'elles ont de la vraisemblance' (Livre II, chap. 2; 6, pp.76-77).

Corneille certainly believed that, once under way, a tragedy's plot should have a compelling inner logic. The dramatist's treatment of a chosen subject had to be *vraisemblable*, with a structure and characterisation which were entirely plausible, but the initial starting-point, the subject of the play, could, indeed preferably should, have a degree of improbability. Historical topics, where truth might be stranger than fiction and of great interest to the audience, were therefore quite acceptable to him. The story of Augustus, with his long and varied career, was ideal material. But, in order to give himself room to manœuvre, to allow the addition of non-historical but psychologically convincing and consistent details, Corneille chose a novel perspective on the famous emperor, a minor aspect of a major topic, namely Cinna's recorded but unexplained conspiracy.

As we have seen, Corneille deemed love an essential but secondary ingredient of tragic plots. Whatever its proportions, it and the other aspects were best contained within a family or other close-knit group. The tighter the relationships of blood, marriage or friendship, the greater the effect of conflict, the more pressing the dilemmas. Within *Cinna* we have a married couple, a pair of lovers, and an unrequited lover. But Emilie, 'la fille d'un Proscrit' (line 72), is treated by Auguste as his adoptive daughter, a replacement for Julie, while it is not fanciful to suggest that the Emperor looks on Cinna and Maxime as his spiritual sons. He, too, is conscious of a debt to his own adoptive father, (Jules) César.

The second *Discours* outlines what Corneille sees as the four possible tragic situations and relationships. Following Aristotle in his *Poetics*, he describes two kinds of plot in which the identity of the intended victim is known to the perpetrators. In one, the deed is carried out as planned, while in the other the contemplated action is not undertaken, or is started but not completed. The other two structures concern characters acting without knowledge of their victims and either going ahead with the deed, discovering the identity later, or realising the identity in time to draw back from the action (*1*, III, p.152).

Aristotle's preference was for these last two plots, where criminal deeds were undertaken or contemplated by characters unaware of the identity of their victims. Oedipus is a good example of the former, while Euripides's Iphigenia recognises her brother Orestes in time. Significantly, Corneille rejects stories with unknown physical identities and comes out clearly in favour of those in which characters act with full knowledge of the facts, carrying out their plans or being prevented from doing so fully, as the case may be. His *Médée*, performed in 1634-35, exemplifies the type of plot in which an action is contemplated and performed: Medea exacts revenge on Jason by killing their two children. *Horace* and *Polyeucte* also fit this pattern. *Cinna* is only one of several Cornelian plays which have characters, with knowledge, beginning to act but denied completion of their deed. Others prior to 1660, as Corneille says, include *Le Cid*, *Rodogune*, *Héraclius* and *Nicomède*.

While it is significant that Corneille does not favour plots depending on discovery of material identity, too close for his liking to the flavour of *romanesque* tragicomedy or pastoral drama, the preference he shows for characters acting with full knowledge of the status and relationship of their victims tells us much about his idea of the tragic. 'Lorsqu'on agit à visage découvert, et qu'on sait à qui on en veut', he says in the second *Discours*, 'le combat des passions contre la nature, ou du devoir contre l'amour, occupe la meilleure partie du poème, et de là naissent les grandes et fortes émotions, qui renouvellent à tous moments, et redoublent la commisération' (*1*, III, p.154). The emotion of pity which, along with fear, constituted the cathartic response for Aristotle could only be aroused by the struggle of feelings against natural instincts (occasioned by knowledge of the persons involved), or by a clash of ideals such as duty and love (again dependent on awareness of identity).

Characters who act knowingly and carry out their deed as planned fare well or badly at the end of the play. Médée rides off triumphantly in her dragon-drawn chariot and Polyeucte's martyrdom results in several conversions to Christianity, whereas Horace, although victorious in battle and pardoned for the murder of his sister, remains an isolated, misunderstood figure as the curtain falls. On the other hand, what possible tragic effect can be aroused when plans go awry and actions have to be aborted, resulting in an absence of death and a 'happy ending'? Corneille describes the situation of such protagonists thus: 'quand ils y font de leur côté tout ce qu'ils peuvent, et qu'ils sont empêchés d'en venir à l'effet par quelque puissance supérieure, ou par quelque changement de fortune qui les fait périr eux-mêmes, ou les réduit sous le pouvoir de ceux qu'ils voulaient perdre, il est hors de doute que cela fait une tragédie d'un genre peut-être plus sublime, que les trois qu'Aristote avoue' (*1*, III, p.153). In other words, what counts most is not the outcome but the process. Events beyond the control of the participants may intervene, either from on high ('par quelque puissance supérieure') or as a result of human action which causes their own death or their subjection to the intended victim. This last possibility is what happens in *Cinna*, with its reversal of fortune in which the conspirators become dependent on the man they sought to kill. But whatever prevents the realisation of a plan does not, should not, destroy the effort put in, the validity of the struggle up until then. It is the wholehearted quality of this struggle against all the odds which counts, not its success or otherwise.

While Corneille accepted Aristotle's well-known definition of the typical tragic character, a person of middling virtue, 'not pre-eminently virtuous and just, whose misfortune, however, is brought upon him not by vice and depravity, but by some error of judgement', he had difficulty in fitting this description even to examples which Aristotle quoted. For the dramatist, such a person certainly creates pity, but he is unsure about the existence of fear. In the case of plays where characters fight to the best of their ability against sometimes overwhelming odds, the effect is to arouse in audience or reader, not just the standard emotions of fear and pity (fear that there but for the grace of God go we, and pity for the plight which the characters face), but something which is 'plus sublime', what Corneille calls *admiration*.

This is not 'admiration' in the conventional seventeenth-century and modern sense of an expression by the audience of its moral approval. Rather Corneille intends to arouse feelings of wonder, awe, amazement, the meaning of the Latin word *admiratio*. In the *Au lecteur* to his tragedy *Nicomède*, published in 1651, Corneille writes: 'Le succès a montré que la fermeté des grands cœurs, qui n'excite que de l'admiration dans l'âme du spectateur, est quelquefois aussi agréable, que la compassion que notre art nous commande de mendier pour leurs misères' (*1*, II, p.641). In 1660 he added in his *Examen* to the play: 'Dans l'admiration qu'on a pour sa [Nicomède's] vertu, je trouve une manière de purger les passions, dont n'a point parlé Aristote, et qui est peut-être plus sûre que celle qu'il prescrit à la tragédie par le moyen de la pitié et de la crainte' (*1*, II, p.643).

Unlike Aristotle, for whom pity and fear were complementary emotions and necessarily linked, Corneille believed that some of his guiltless characters would arouse pity but no fear in the audience or reader, 'puisque nous les y voyons opprimés, et près de périr, sans aucune faute de leur part, dont nous puissions nous corriger sur leur exemple' (second *Discours*; *1*, III, p.147). From the possibility of pity without any accompanying fear it is but a short step to believing that certain figures stir up in us a less negative feeling, amazement for their achievements against the odds, the wonder which is *admiration*.

Importantly, this audience response can apply both to good and to evil characters. 'Cléopâtre dans *Rodogune* est très méchante', Corneille writes in the first *Discours*, 'il n'y a point de parricide qui lui fasse horreur, pourvu qu'il la puisse conserver sur un trône qu'elle préfère à toutes choses, tant son attachement à la domination est violent; mais tous ses crimes sont accompagnés d'une grandeur d'âme, qui a quelque chose de si haut, qu'en même temps qu'on déteste ses actions, on admire la source dont elles partent' (*1*, III, p.129). Like his earlier Médée, the Syrian queen in the 1644-45 tragedy is evil, but in Corneille's eyes she has a 'goodness of character' appropriate to her circumstances. Strict morality is not an issue in our response to Cléopâtre, an unscrupulous woman who will do anything, including killing her own two sons, in order to retain power until, cornered, she drinks the poison which has already been used to despatch one of them and dies unrepentant.

In all of Corneille's tragedies, whether death is present or not, the tragic atmosphere is largely dependent on the extent to which individual characters reach an understanding of their situation. If discovery of physical identity is rejected as melodramatic, recognition of guilt or achievement of knowledge are quite different matters. This is another reason why *Cinna* cannot end with Auguste's act of clemency, for its effect on the others and their reaction to it are an essential part of the tragedy. Despite the general truth of the statement that, in *Cinna*, 'on sait à qui on en veut', there are significant gaps in all the characters' awareness of what is going on. When Livie appears in Act IV, she seems unaware of, or is certainly unresponsive to, her husband's inner turmoil. Until enlightened in the second interval, Maxime does not realise that Cinna and Emilie are in love or that Emilie, who he thought loved Auguste as a father (line 702), is the instigator of the conspiracy. Euphorbe has been oblivious of his master Maxime's love for Emilie (line 721), just as Emilie herself has been. Cinna only learns of Maxime's amorous rivalry (and hence the source of the betrayal) in Act V, Scene 3, the answer to the question he was asking himself while Auguste was upbraiding him (ll.1543-44). Auguste above all, despite his closeness to Emilie, Cinna and Maxime, has no inkling of the assassination plans being made against him. The plausibility of these gaps in knowledge may vary, some of them at least being accepted by us as very natural human failings.

A similar but different problem afflicts Cinna and Emilie. They do not lack essential knowledge but initially are unwilling to recognise certain facts of which they are reminded, above all the change which has already taken place within Auguste. This wilful blindness, like the ignorance of others, is a further source of dramatic irony for the audience which, throughout the play, is in a privileged position, not shared by any character, of witnessing all events, every conversation, and of anticipating, or failing to anticipate, the outcomes.

The clemency of Auguste was Corneille's *terminus ad quem*, for the historians confirmed it as the result of the conspiracy and he had deliberately included it as a subtitle when the play was initially performed and printed. But where the dramatist was free to invent was in the means used to reach that end and, to a lesser extent, in the attitudes of other persons involved in the unexpected pardon, especially the unhistorical Emilie and Maxime. By choosing a subject which was *vrai* but conveniently underdocumented, Corneille granted himself much discretion in the establishment of supporting cast and in the extent of their description. It is often said that psychological plausibility is of secondary importance in drama, which bears only a passing resemblance to real life. Earlier sections of this study have sought to bring out the specific needs of a performed text, the constraints of staging as well as the freedom of the playwright to choose and sequence his events. Yet while no play can possibly convey a fully realistic picture of events or description of character, the best seem to achieve a roundedness of characterisation which convinces by its closeness to what we understand of human motivations and actions.

Corneille's additions to historical *vérité* had to be at least *vraisemblables* if they were to fit seamlessly into the rather meagre framework of known facts. The second *Discours* suggests that Cinna's conspiracy against Auguste was a necessary consequence of his love for Emilie, since the latter had success in the former as a prerequisite. The conspiracy is true, the love is merely *vraisemblable,* plausible, but there is a necessary linkage between one and the other. Likewise, says Corneille, Cinna's remorse and indecision are but a *vraisemblable* result of Auguste's goodness, and here the link, too, is merely plausible rather than necessary, since Cinna's response could be quite different from what it is in the play. Finally, his meeting with Emilie in Act III is unhistorical (since she herself is an invented character), but, although only a credible scene, it is a necessary consequence of his love for her, since her opinion about the possible dropping of the conspiracy is essential. Here, Corneille points out, is the case of a necessary connection between two merely plausible circumstances (*1*, III, pp.165-66).

These interesting theoretical discussions throw much light on the care which Corneille took to marshal and, if necessary, create events and characters which had sufficient linkages and motivations to produce psychologically convincing situations, without which the plot of the play could not move forward. In addition, most of his tragedies achieve this result without any outside intervention. Corneille's main interest in tragedy lies in the interaction of a number of persons depicting various aspects of the human condition and its development through action, rather than (as Racine will do later) exploring the inner workings of individuals and their struggle with inevitable catastrophe. Given their ability to choose, Cornelian characters operate as relatively free, self-sufficient agents within a carefully defined social group, susceptible to all the constraints and to the successes or failures which such a body may produce, able to accept and boast about the happy outcomes but, by the same token, forced to accept responsibility for their failures. They conflict with one another in a specific political or historical situation, whereas Racinian heroes and heroines cannot fulfil themselves individually owing to an inherent flaw of character or inability to reconcile mutually incompatible characteristics and thus produce in the audience the Aristotelian tragic emotions of pity and fear (or, rather, pity-and-fear).

Of course there are quite frequent references in *Cinna* to *le ciel / les cieux*, to *les dieux*, to *le destin / les destinées*, and to *le sort*. It is tempting to fall back on one or more of these supernatural elements to explain not just the final clemency but the almost superhuman forcefulness of the chief conspirators or perhaps Emilie's feelings of repose even amidst the greatest of dangers. Tempting but mistaken, for, compared with other of his plays, the role of outside forces is very limited. The supernatural has a significant part in *Médée*, where Jason, unable to punish his murderous wife, invokes the gods as the only possible remaining source of revenge just before he commits suicide. In the much more down-to-earth *Horace*, destiny plays a major role, expressed through the presence of the gods and the inscrutability of their purposes. If Horace can meet the challenge which they set, he will be truly fulfilled. His sister Camille consults an oracle which predicts, ironically as it turns out, that her wishes will be granted and that she will be united to her lover Curiace (in marriage, as she hopes, but in death as events later prove). Christian martyr plays such as *Polyeucte* or *Théodore* (performed in 1645-46) contain major elements of divine intervention much closer in nature to the experiences or beliefs of seventeenth-century French audiences.

In *Cinna*, on the other hand, the terms mentioned above are used very largely to inject an element of appropriate local colour, the need for which was less widely felt at the time than it is today. The stage treatment of pagan society raised particular difficulties, although there were solutions such as avoiding named divinities and consistently using the plural *les Dieux* (with or without a capital) to distinguish the concept from that familiar to the Christian audience and yet maintain a discreet intellectual link to *Dieu* and to the widely acknowledged concept of the divine right of kings.

Le Ciel, used over twenty times in the text, is often simply a euphemism for *le hasard*, as when Emilie tells Auguste in Act V that 'le Ciel rompt le succès [= outcome] que je m'étais promis' (line 1580, cf. ll.1461-62). The same word covers a range of concepts such as history (ll.1003-04), the future (line 257), fortune (line 1145), events in general (ll.1293, 1663), or favourable circumstances (ll.1327, 1348). At times it could be replaced by the pronoun *on* (ll.165, 657), while on other occasions a different construction would be substituted in modern French (ll.925-26). The plural *Cieux* also has general connotations, as seen conveniently in the sequence 'cet ordre des Cieux' (line 547), 'l'ordre céleste'(line 557), and 'un ordre des Dieux' (line 559), similar to 'l'ordre du Destin' (line 389), and all summed up in Emilie's phrase 'l'ordre de tout le Monde' (line 942), i.e. 'l'ordre du monde entier'. Of course, specific reference to the gods is present in Livie's statement to her husband that 'le Ciel [vous prépare] une place entre les Immortels' (line 1772), but this is part of the final process of deification of the Emperor described in history and of the prophetic powers of Livie.

If space allowed, a similar analysis could be made of references in *Cinna* to *le sort* or *la fortune* and to further examples of *Dieux* and *Destin*, occurring within the line or at the rhyme where they attract suitable pair-words such as *assassin* or *mort* and are perhaps introduced for that purpose. All such references to supernatural influences form part, I would suggest, of Corneille's need to include an element of early Rome in his play without hurting the sensibilities of his contemporary audience. But in one case interpretation of *le Ciel* is of particular importance. In his scene with Livie, having rejected his wife's opportunist advice, Auguste says impatiently 'Le Ciel m'inspirera ce qu'ici je dois faire' (line 1258). Critics who see the dénouement as the result of the intervention of divine grace use this line as one of their key proofs. However, in the light of the analyses above, I believe that we should compare the Emperor's words with, say, Euphorbe's comments to Maxime in Act III. There the *affranchi* has to respond to his master's impossible requests, dismissing the insistent questions with 'Et du reste, le temps en pourra disposer' (line 784) and 'J'espère, toutefois qu'à force d'y rêver...' (line 791). The characters are different, but the mood is a similar one of irritation: Euphorbe and Auguste both want to get rid of their interlocutors and make use of the first hackneyed phrases which come to mind.

If, as I would maintain, the clemency is an instinctive gesture on Auguste's part, coming as unexpectedly to him as it does to the conspirators and to us, it is clear that all the main characters in the play have, of their own accord, arrived at a recognition or realisation of their true situation. Maxime, who has been the most active during the five acts, consulting with Auguste, arguing with Cinna, seeking solutions with Euphorbe, expressing love to Emilie and inventing both a feigned death and a highly coloured abduction plan, has his life spared, but his jealousy may remain alive. Cinna's plotting is transformed into devotion to the Emperor which will withstand, he says, the heavens falling. Emilie is illuminated by Auguste's 'hautes bontés' and this outward acceptance is confirmed by an inner conviction (line 1720). The conspirators have indeed done all in their power: as Emilie puts it while apostrophising Rome and her late father in Act IV, 'J'ai fait de mon côté tout ce que j'ai pu faire' (line 1306). A material event or change of circumstances (Maxime's betrayal) renders them powerless; an inner conviction, born of Auguste's magnanimity, allows them to destroy their now outdated hatred (or hatreds, for Maxime's is different from that of Cinna and Emilie) and come to a reconciliation based on an acceptance of the worth of the new situation in which they find themselves.

In order to arrive at this final recognition, characters have followed different routes, coming from different starting-points and travelling at different speeds. Auguste is ready for a radical change before the curtain goes up but has difficulty in knowing how and when to achieve it. Emilie and Cinna have been in love for over four years and plotting recently, yet their itineraries within the five acts of the play vary considerably, with Cinna experiencing doubts while Emilie remains steadfast to her original plan. Maxime appears more detached, a co-conspirator recruited for the 'right reason', the downfall of the Emperor and perhaps the Empire, yet revealed late on as having personal motives as well. These separate tracks through the action of the play and the changes which each character undergoes provide its variety but also its cohesiveness. Similarly, the emotions aroused in us, and indeed in the stage characters too at times, are wide-ranging yet coherent: we feel pity for the plight of Auguste (not Octave) and perhaps even of the unfortunate Maxime, we fear for the conspirators and for the well-being of the distraught Auguste, and finally we experience that overwhelming sense of amazement and wonder at Auguste's unconditional pardon and the accused's ready and wholesale acceptance of it. That emotion, and the happy ending which accompanies it, constitute tragedy in Corneille's terms, 'une espèce de nouvelle tragédie plus belle que les trois qu'[Aristote] recommande, et qu'il leur eût sans doute préférée, s'il l'eût connue' (second *Discours*; *1*, III, pp.153-54).

6. Sources and Background

It is not by chance that, in a brief study of *Cinna*, this is the shortest chapter, and the last. For the guiding principle behind the earlier sections has been to emphasise that Corneille wrote plays, not moral tracts, or studies (fortuitously in verse) of how his various characters pursued values which offered an indirect commentary on the political situation in early modern France.

Attempts by influential critics, particularly Georges Couton, to see the source of Corneille's tragedies in specific events of contemporary French history have been profoundly misguided. For they simply fail to produce an agreed result but spend much time looking for one amid a series of peasant rebellions and aristocratic plots against the State which certainly existed and with which Corneille must have been familiar. Thus *Cinna* is said variously to have been a response to the 'Conspiration des Dames' (1626), the 'Journée des Dupes' (1630), the Montmorency affair (1632), the arrest of Puylaurens (1635), the 'Sédition des Va-Nu-Pieds' (1639-40), the pardoning of the Duc de Vendôme (1641), the plot led by the Comte de Soissons (1641), or the conspiracy of Cinq-Mars and de Thou, executed in Lyons in September 1642. The hunt for parallels in history and politics inevitably distorts the qualities inherent in the plays themselves. Corneille wrote for the theatre, and although not an actor or director himself, showed early on an intuitive grasp of the needs of the stage. His tragedies, based on historical details but always going well beyond them, have their own momentum and dynamism, dictated in part by his imagination, in part also by the requirements of the genre as understood in his day.

This is not to deny that Corneille, like his fellow-writers, was influenced by the happenings and personalities of his time, including the social unrest caused by high taxation, plague and famine, resistance by the nobility to the forces of a centralising monarchy, and the harsh repression which greeted dissent at all levels. But it is one thing to say that the assumptions or ideas of characters in *Cinna* bear the stamp of Louis XIII's reign and of the methods of his chief minister Richelieu; it is quite another to see the play as a deliberate, direct comment or attack on the royal handling of any particular element of insurrection. The concepts of history and of historical perspective being less developed then than now, it is not surprising if seventeenth-century playwrights, Corneille among them, visualised moments in ancient history or myth through the mirror of contemporary events and relationships which had some resemblance to them. It is dangerously reductive, however, to go beyond this very general level of manipulation.

Where we are on safer and more useful ground is in looking briefly at earlier and contemporary written sources. Like all tragedy writers of his day, Corneille drew on historians' accounts both ancient and modern, French plays on similar subjects, and other prose writing of the period, as well as his own imagination. Roman history provided the France of Louis XIII and XIV with centuries of examples to exploit, a range of political systems to praise or criticise, figures major and minor to incorporate into different kinds of plays. Like his audiences, he would have been familiar with recent compilations in French such as the *Histoire romaine* by Scipion Dupleix, which first appeared in 1637, or Nicolas Coëffeteau's *Histoire romaine*, published in Paris in 1621 and reprinted fifty times in the next sixty years. But, in addition to Coëffeteau, he went back to the original sources, incorporating into editions of *Cinna* from 1643 to 1657 an extract from Seneca's *De clementia* accompanied, until 1646 only, by the paraphrase of most of it given in Book I of Montaigne's *Essais* (1580).

Writing in AD 55 or 56 to the young Nero, Seneca recounts in chapter 9 of Book I the betrayal of the conspiracy by one of the accomplices, Augustus's contradictory thoughts during a largely sleepless night, and Livia's intervention, followed by his acceptance of her advice ('Happy to have found a supporter, he thanked his wife ...') and a more than two-hour interrogation of Cinna, ending with clemency, friendship and, later, the consulship. Seneca sets the

incident in Gaul, not Rome, and around 16-13 BC, when the
Emperor would have been well into his reign (27 BC-AD 14). Earlier
in Book I, he comments more generally on the notion of clemency,
suggesting that pardoning should not be a common occurrence, for
confusion and an epidemic of vice can arise if the distinction
between good and evil is removed. A wise moderation should be
observed, based on distinguishing curable from hopeless individuals
(I.2.2). Great power confers grace and glory only when it is
beneficial; of all men none is better suited to mercy than a king or a
prince (I.3.3). While repeated punishment may crush the hatred of a
few, it stirs the hatred of all. By exercising mercy, kings gain a sense
of security unknown to lesser mortals (I.8.6).

Not acknowledged by Corneille are the contributions of
Appian and Cassius Dio. The 2nd-century AD Greek writer Appian
gives a detailed account in Book IV of his *Roman History* of the
proscriptions under Antony, Lepidus and Octavian and mentions
Thoranius, said by some to have been a tutor of Octavius (IV.3.12).
Shortly afterwards he lists a different Thuranius, who was also
named for death and betrayed by his own son. The father then asked
to see his daughter to warn her against her brother's treachery
(IV.4.18). Corneille conflates the two references and comes up with
his Toranius, tutor or guardian of Octave, and the daughter, whom he
names Emilie. The *Roman History* of the 3rd-century AD Greek
writer Cassius Dio includes a very long account (LII.1-41) of
Augustus's meeting with his counsellors Agrippa and Maecenas
which took place in 29 BC and inspired Corneille's Act II
deliberation scene. Book XLVII also describes the proscriptions,
while Book LV gives an account of Gnaeus Cornelius Cinna
Magnus's conspiracy, set in AD 4 (a year before Cinna's consulship)
and in Rome rather than Gaul, and not said to be betrayed by a
fellow-conspirator. Livia engages in a lengthy discussion with her
husband (LV.14-21) which Corneille greatly reduces in his Act IV,
Scene 3.

In *Cinna*, historical references go back to Numa Pompilius
(715-673? BC), the second of the seven kings of Rome (line 556)
and, more specifically, some five hundred years before the action of

the play (line 523), to the fall of the last of the Tarquins (line 561), Tarquinius Superbus, in 509 BC. Rome's hatred of kings (ll.481-88, 523-25) and its wars against external kings (ll.529-33) are seen as cogent arguments against a monarchical imperial system. The late republic is represented by Sulla (138-78 BC), his rivalry with Marius (ll.581-83), and his principate (82-79 BC), and is compared with that of Caesar, especially since Sulla died 'happily' after retirement (ll.381-82), whereas Caesar gained legitimacy, struggled against Pompey and, after the latter's death, became the victim of an assassination (line 384) which haunts his successor Auguste. However it is not just Octave/Auguste who has earlier parallels to think about. Caesar's murderers Brutus and Cassius are seen by Emilie as the last Romans worthy of the name (line 268), but are attacked by Maxime for having caused the ascent of the tyrant Auguste (ll.665-68) and by Cinna (ll.669-70), who adds that Brutus in particular had hesitated because of remorse (ll.829-32).

Finally, many French dramatic writers of the 1630s and 1640s chose to depict tragic episodes from the history of ancient Rome: the rape of Lucretia (Du Ryer, Chapoton), the deaths of Pompey (Chaulmer, Corneille), Mithridates (La Calprenède), Brutus and Portia (Guérin de Bouscal), Mariamne (Tristan L'Hermite), Antony and Cleopatra (Mairet), Scipio (Desmarets de Saint-Sorlin), Seneca (Tristan L'Hermite), and Scaevola (Du Ryer), to name but some of the best-known. Corneille himself went back to legendary, pre-historical Rome in *Horace*, and to Roman politics outside Italy in *Polyeucte*, set in Armenia in the 3rd century AD, and in *Nicomède* (1650-51), which shows the Romans in 2nd-century Bithynia. He drew indirect inspiration from many of his predecessors and more directly from Georges de Scudéry's *La Mort de César* of 1635, as Jean Mesnard has shown (*33*). Scudéry, a leading critic of *Le Cid* in 1637, depicts the events which culminated in Caesar's murder in 44 BC. As noted already, his tragedy is structurally and dramatically inferior to *Cinna*. But, as well as dipping into the general pool of vocabulary and conventional images associated with conspiracies and assassinations, Corneille seems to have been inspired by some of

Scudéry's lines: lines 1-5, 18-20, 45-46, and 163-66 of *Cinna* recall
La Mort de César, 867-71, 880-82, 883, and 603-08 respectively.

Seventeenth-century playwrights saw no indignity in
rehandling themes treated by earlier dramatists or even their very
contemporaries. For improvement of often-worked material
considered as a common source was, in some senses, deemed a
greater achievement than producing an entirely new subject.
Similarly, writers of tragedy returned to ancient history or myth for
their inspiration, choosing incidents and characters and then altering
and adding greatly to them for the purposes of their plots. Corneille
selected and merged details from Seneca, Cassius Dio and probably
Appian, changing dates and inventing characters and thereby motives
to fill out an undetailed account. His Auguste claims to have reigned
for twenty years (line 1248); Cassius Dio's account would make the
reign over thirty years, while Seneca's conspiracy date brings it
down to eleven to fourteen years only. The Emperor would be some
sixty-seven years old, had Corneille followed Cassius Dio exactly, or
between forty-seven and fifty according to Seneca. History tells us
that the fall of Julia, Augustus's daughter, happened in 2 BC,
whereas the play suggests (line 1589) that her exile took place before
his adoption of Emilie. There is nothing unusual in this melding of
events and characters and their rearrangement into a different pattern
by the dramatist, more especially since this is the first French stage
treatment of the story and details of the actual conspiracy are
sketchy. 'Rien n'y contredit l'Histoire, bien que beaucoup de choses
y soient ajoutées', as Corneille puts it in the 1660 *Examen* (*1*, I,
p.910). He adds that the changes and additions produce a play with
an *intrigue* which is nonetheless *simple*, not *implexe* or complicated
like those of *Rodogune* or *Héraclius* a year or two later. Despite his
own liking for complex plots, the result is that in *Cinna* 'la facilité de
concevoir le Sujet, qui n'est ni trop chargé d'incidents, ni trop
embarrassé des récits de ce qui s'est passé avant le commencement
de la Pièce, est une des causes sans doute de la grande approbation
qu'il a reçue' (*1*, I, p.912).

Bibliography

Listed here are primary texts and secondary works referred to elsewhere in the volume or which have been of particular use in its preparation.

PRIMARY TEXTS

Editions of Cinna:

1. Corneille, *Œuvres complètes,* ed. by G. Couton, 3 vols, Paris, Gallimard, 1980-87 (Bibliothèque de la Pléiade). Vol.1 reproduces the final (1682) text of *Cinna.*
2. ——, *Théâtre complet,* ed. by A. Niderst, 3 parts in 6 vols, Rouen, Editions de l'Université de Rouen, 1984-86. Vol.2 of the first part reproduces the original (1643) text of *Cinna.*
3. ——, *Cinna,* mise en scène et commentaires de Charles Dullin, Paris, Seuil, 1948
4. ——, *Cinna,* ed. by D.A. Watts, London, University of London Press, 1964
5. ——, *Cinna,* ed. by G. Forestier, Paris, Gallimard, 1994 (Coll. Folio Théâtre)

Other 17th- and 18th-century texts:

6. Aubignac, F. Hédelin, abbé d', *La Pratique du théâtre*, ed. by P. Martino, Algiers, Carbonel, and Paris, Champion, 1927
7. Corneille, *Writings on the Theatre*, ed. by H.T. Barnwell, Oxford, Blackwell, 1965
8. Scudéry, G. de, *La Mort de César*, in Scudéry, *'Le Prince déguisé' et 'La Mort de César'*, ed. by E. Dutertre and D. Moncond'Huy, Paris, STFM, 1992
9. Voltaire, *Commentaires sur Corneille*, ed. by D. Williams, in *Les Œuvres complètes de Voltaire/The Complete Works of Voltaire*, ed. by G. Barber et al., vols 53-55, Banbury, Voltaire Foundation, 1974-75. The comments on *Cinna* are in vol.54.

SECONDARY WORKS

10. Barnwell, H.T., *The Tragic Drama of Corneille and Racine: an old parallel revisited*, Oxford, Clarendon Press, 1982
11. Bénichou, P., *Morales du grand siècle*, Paris, Gallimard, 1948
12. Clarke, D.R., 'Heroic Prudence and Reason in the Seventeenth Century: Auguste's pardon of Cinna', *Forum for Modern Language Studies*, 1 (1965), 328-38
13. ——, *Pierre Corneille: poetics and political drama under Louis XIII*, Cambridge, Cambridge University Press, 1992
14. Couton, G., *Corneille*, Paris, Hatier, 1958
15. Descotes, M., *Les Grands Rôles du théâtre de Corneille*, Paris, PUF, 1962
16. Doubrovsky, S., *Corneille et la dialectique du héros*, Paris, Gallimard, 1964
17. Forestier, G., *Essai de génétique théâtrale: Corneille à l'œuvre*, Paris, Klincksieck, 1996
18. Fumaroli, M., *L'Age de l'éloquence*, Geneva, Droz, 1980
19. ——, *Héros et orateurs: rhétorique et dramaturgie cornéliennes*, Geneva, Droz, 1990
20. Georges, A., 'La Conversion d'Emilie dans *Cinna*', *L'Information littéraire*, 36 (1984), 121-28
21. Gossip, C.J., *An Introduction to French Classical Tragedy*, London, Macmillan, 1981
22. ——, 'La Clémence d'Auguste, ou pour une interprétation textuelle du *Cinna* de Corneille', *XVIIe Siècle*, 46 (1994), 547-53
23. ——, 'Potentialité et actualisation chez Corneille: remarques sur la clémence d'Auguste', *Papers on French Seventeenth Century Literature*, 47 (1997), 1-9
24. Greenberg, M., *Corneille, Classicism and the Rules of Symmetry*, Cambridge, Cambridge University Press, 1986
25. Harwood-Gordon, S., *The Poetic Style of Corneille's Tragedies: an aesthetic interpretation*, Lewiston / Lampeter / Queenston, Edwin Mellen Press, 1989
26. Herland, L., *Cinna, ou le péché et la grâce: fragments inédits*, texte établi et présenté par Simone Dosmond, Toulouse, Publications de l'Université de Toulouse-Le Mirail, 1984
27. Jasinski, R., 'Sur *Cinna*', *Europe*, 540-541 (avril-mai 1974), 114-30
28. Lasserre, F., *Corneille de 1638 à 1642: la crise technique d'*'Horace', '*Cinna*' et '*Polyeucte*', Paris / Seattle / Tübingen, PFSCL, 1990
29. Leiner, W., and Bayne, S., '*Cinna* ou l'agenouillement d'Emilie devant la clémence d'Auguste', in *Onze études sur l'image de la femme dans la littérature du XVIIe siècle*, ed. by W. Leiner, Tübingen, G. Narr, and Paris, J.-M. Place, 1978, 195-219

30. Lyons, J.D., *The Tragedy of Origins: Pierre Corneille and historical perspectives,* Stanford, Stanford University Press, 1996
31. Maurens, J., *La Tragédie sans tragique: le néo-stoïcisme dans l'œuvre de Pierre Corneille,* Paris, A. Colin, 1966
32. May, G., *Tragédie cornélienne, tragédie racinienne: étude sur les sources de l'intérêt dramatique,* Urbana, University of Illinois Press, 1948
33. Mesnard, J., 'Le Thème de la mort de César dans *Cinna',* in *Mélanges Jeanne Lods,* Paris, ENS de Jeunes Filles, 1978, 707-26
34. Mongrédien, G., *Recueil des textes et des documents du XVIIe siècle relatifs à Corneille,* Paris, CNRS, 1972
35. Mourgues, O. de, 'Coherence and Incoherence in Cinna', in *Form and Meaning: aesthetic coherence in seventeenth-century French drama. Studies presented to Harry Barnwell,* ed. by W. D. Howarth et al., Amersham, Avebury, 1982, 51-62
36. Nadal, O., *Le Sentiment de l'amour dans l'œuvre de P. Corneille,* Paris, Gallimard, 1948
37. Nelson, R.J., 'Kinship and Kingship in *Cinna', Forum for Modern Language Studies,* 1 (1965), 311-27
38. Pavel, T.G., *La Syntaxe narrative des tragédies de Corneille. Recherches et perspectives,* Paris, Klincksieck, 1976
39. Phillips, H., 'Corneille: Ethic and *Polis'* in *Ethics and Politics in Seventeenth-Century France: essays in honour of Derek A. Watts,* ed. by K. Cameron and E. Woodrough, Exeter, University of Exeter Press, 1996, 163-73
40. Pintard, R., 'Autour de *Cinna* et de *Polyeucte*: nouveaux problèmes de chronologie et de critique cornéliennes', *Revue d'histoire littéraire de la France,* 64 (1964), 377-413
41. Poirier, G., *Corneille et la vertu de prudence,* Geneva, Droz, 1984
42. Prigent, M., *Le Héros et l'état dans la tragédie de P. Corneille,* Paris, PUF, 1986
43. Quémada, B., ed., *P. Corneille: 'Cinna'. Concordances, index et relevés statistiques,* Paris, Larousse, 1971
44. Stegmann, A., *L'Héroïsme cornélien: genèse et signification,* 2 vols, Paris, A. Colin, 1968
45. Sutcliffe, F.E., 'Le Pardon d'Auguste: politique et morale dans *Cinna'* in *Modern Miscellany Presented to Eugène Vinaver,* ed. by T.E. Lawrenson et al., Manchester, Manchester University Press, 1969, 243-53
46. Sweetser, M.-O., *La Dramaturgie de Corneille,* Geneva, Droz, 1977
47. Tiefenbrun, S.W., 'The Big Switch: a study of *Cinna*'s reversals' in *Signs of the Hidden: semiotic studies,* Amsterdam, Rodopi, 1980, 181-208

48. Yarrow, P.J., 'Réflexions sur le dénouement de *Cinna*', *Papers on French Seventeenth Century Literature*, 21 (1984), 547-58
49. Zuber, R., 'La Conversion d'Emilie', in *Héroïsme et création littéraire sous les règnes d'Henri IV et Louis XIII*, ed. by N. Hepp and G. Livet, Paris, Klincksieck, 1974, 261-76

CRITICAL GUIDES TO FRENCH TEXTS

edited by

Roger Little, Wolfgang van Emden, David Williams